In Search of BPM Excellence

Founded in 1992, The Business Process Management Group (BPMG), is a global business club exchanging ideas and best practice in business process and change management. We have over 10,000 members in 124 countries, across all business sectors. Through case studies, seminars, education and research, we support our members in improving their organizations' work across business processes, information technology, and, most importantly, people.

www.bpmg.org

In Search of BPM Excellence

Straight from the Thought Leaders

The Business Process Management Group

Contributing authors:
Steve Towers
Roger Burlton
Peter Fingar
Andrew Spanyi
Vasile Buciuman-Coman
Adrian George Sahlean
Mark McGregor
Dr. Pehong Chen
Ronald Ross
Jorge Eduardo Soares Coelho
Terry Schurter
David Lyneham-Brown
Keith Harrison-Broninski
Michael McClellan
Martyn Ould

Meghan-Kiffer Press
Tampa, Florida, USA, www.mkpress.com
Innovation at the Intersection of Business and Technology

Publisher's Cataloging-in-Publication Data
Business Process Management Group
In Search of BPM Excellence : Straight from the Thought Leaders / Business Process Management Group, - 1st ed.
p. cm.
Includes bibliographic references.
ISBN 0-929652-40-1 (paperback)
1. Management 2. Technological innovation. 3. Strategic planning. 4. Management information systems. 5. Information technology. 6. Information resources management. 7. Organizational change.

HF58.8..B464 2005   LC Control# 2005922618

658.8'00285-dc21   CIP

Published by Meghan-Kiffer Press
310 East Fern Street — Suite G
Tampa, FL 33604 USA

Any product mentioned in this book may be a trademark of its company.

Meghan-Kiffer books are available at special quantity discounts for corporate education and training use. For more information write Special Sales, Meghan-Kiffer Press, Suite G, 310 East Fern Street, Tampa, Florida 33604 or email mkpress@tampabay.rr.com

MK
Meghan-Kiffer Press
Tampa, Florida, USA
Publishers of Advanced Business-Technology Books for Competitive Advantage
Printed in the United States of America.   SAN 249-7980
MK Printing 10 9 8 7 6 5 4 3 2 1

Dedicated to the operation of business as a sustainable and repeatable behavior that retains competitive advantages, and maintains corporate health despite the every increasing pace of change in the global economy.

"We are what we repeatedly do. Excellence, therefore, is not an act but a habit."
—Aristotle

"It is not the strongest of the species that survive, nor the most intelligent, but the one most responsive to change."
—Charles Darwin

"The world is changing very fast. Big will not beat small anymore. It will be the fast beating the slow."
—Rupert Murdoch, CEO of News Corporation: Media & Entertainment Company

"Willingness to change is a strength, even if it means plunging part of the company into total confusion for a while."
—Jack Welch, Former Chairman and CEO of General Electric

Table of Contents

Preface

Where do you go to gain insight into this thing called business process management?

- Why is business process management so important and just how important is it?
- What should you be considering when making BPM a reality, as Best Practice? or Next Practice?
- How will you get there and is there a map you can follow that will make sure you get where you want to go?
- Who needs BPM, do I?

These are questions of greatest importance to business people and the Business Process Management Group has tracked down the leading thought leaders, analysts, methodologists and consultants in the field of business process management to get the answers.

BPM sits at the heart of the Business Evolution we have now begun to experience – and that will continue to be a primary economic driver over the next several decades.

This book, *In Search of BPM Excellence*, is for those who want to sustain consistent, ongoing success, profit, and growth of their businesses in the midst of the current sea of change. This is the book for those in search of excellence.

We would like to thank all of the authors for working hard to make this book the insightful collection of information that it is. There is certainly no other book like this and the sweeping scope of *In Search of BPM Excellence* opens the door to insights likely to play out in numerous important decisions and actions for many years.

The Business Process Management Group
March 2005

One

In the Beginning

By Steve Towers

INTRODUCTION: *This short essay by Steve Towers — CEO of The Business Process Management Group — takes an insightful look back into history with the early days of the industrial revolution where, surprisingly, many of the core concepts of BPM that influence what BPM means today were first placed into action by key figures of the revolution through application of rigorous scientific method.*

I was cogitating at a conference recently (you do when it is your third in 10 days) and I was struck by the thought that if someone sent you to a Desert Island, with the usual motley choice of artifacts then what business books would you take?

It isn't such a theoretical issue as the question most often asked of the BPMG. "What book should I read to understand this process stuff?" and of course the answer is many and varied depending on your perspective i.e. strategy, people, process or systems? So I thought (before we answer that question later) let's get back to basics and see what my dog haired tomes consist of in my desert island solitude?

I dredged my slide riddled mind (76 presentations in two weeks is truly taxing) and related my own path to process nirvana. Who influenced my early career as an Industrial Engineer in British Gas? What inspiration put me on the road to process change? Who really laid the foundations of the current extraordinary interest in process and performance?

For my part, I can identify as many major works that each took their place in pragmatic practice across the many organizations generous enough to let me ply my trade. As a practitioner of organization and methods, work-study, business analysis and then systems engineering I searched for inspiration. Later in various management roles with utility companies, financial services (thank you Citibank) and then the dot com boom I would read dozens of books. Some authors offered promises of glittering prizes with new and untested theories, whilst others claimed to provide best practice approaches born of 'leading companies'. Many, like a Chinese meal, left me feeling hungry again shortly later. Other authors were downright dangerous in their proclamations and thankfully passed into the fad graveyard as quickly as they had arrived. Through it all though, I would return again and again to the same volumes. Some writing transcends generations and cultures and provides still fresh inspiration for those willing to delve into their promise and that's what I would like to share.

Naturally, you may have a different choice based on your own explorations however I know my favorites and present them up for discussion in the belief that others may also derive long term sustenance on their journeys to improve and benefit our organizations and people. Explore and enjoy.

In the beginning…some would claim process thinking goes back to the ancient Greeks and is actually mentioned in mythology of that time, including the 'process' of duping with the Trojan Horse. Not being an historian or indeed having much interest in the business practices of ancient civilizations I prefer to regard the beginning of modern thinking and good process practice with the industrial revolution. The first people to really articulate the meaning of process were grappling with mass production and industrialization. Hence the first three writers and practitioners: Frederick Winslow Taylor, Frank Gilbreth and Henry Ford.

The Principles of Scientific Management [1]
–Frederick Winslow Taylor

This book was the first to put 'management' on the map, and its influence on industrialization during the 20th century was enormous. The approach advocated by Taylor became know as 'Taylorism' and has been variously knocked, ridiculed, rejected and reinvented and to this day is the corner stone of a set of thinking and practice known as 'scientific management'.

Based on his work as Chief Engineer at the Midvale Steel Works where Taylor developed detailed systems intended to gain maximum efficiency from both workers and machines in the factory. These systems relied on time and motion studies, which help determine the best methods for performing a task in the least amount of time.

Taylor believed that the secret of productivity was finding the right challenge for each person, then paying him well for increased output. At Midvale, he used time studies to set daily production quotas. Incentives would be paid to those reaching their daily goal. Those who didn't reach their goal would get the differential rate, a much lower pay. Taylor doubled productivity using time study, systematic controls and tools, functional foremanship, and his new wage scheme. He paid the person not the job. Through many roles as an engineering consultant, he refined and improved his approach to improving processes and along the way collected many awards and several enemies who rejected his direct and incisive approach to improving productivity.

Much of his famous book, "The Principles of Scientific Management," was written from transcripts of talks Taylor gave in his later life when reflecting on his trials introducing change and new ways of working. The system he describes in his book is a composite of everything he had learned from trying different things at many companies. Taylor did what he could to fit as much of his thinking to his client's problems and motives for each particular situation. Good consultants use this type of process today. We can now observe that Taylor was the first person in history to make a systematic attempt to improve both productivity (efficiency and effectiveness) and work life in factories.

Motion Study: A Method for Increasing the Efficiency of the Workman [2]
–Frank Gilbreth

Frederick Taylor set the scene for a wave of thinking that brought scientific management to the attention of the leading organizations of the late Victorian era. Involved in this revolution of business thinking were the husband and wife team of Frank and Lilian Gilbreth who were the first to formally link process with measurement. Their fundamental belief was that by analyzing the motion of work you could improve productivity, motivation and safety and through this create the 'win-win' situation leading to higher outputs and better quality of life. The Gilbreths devised sets of measurement through direct study and innovatively the photography of work activity and tasks leading to a detailed understanding of the components of work. These studies were enhanced with a range of tools and techniques, many still used today including the micro chronometer, a timing device which records to $1/2000$ of a second and was placed in the area being photographed. As a result of their analysis the Gilbreths concluded that there were 16 units of movement, subsequently called therbligs (Gilbreth backward and slightly altered for ease of pronunciation). The idea of measurement of performance is fundamental to establishing effective and efficient processes and much is owed to this early work that focused on worker activity and optimum outputs. Although the Gilbreths suffered the usual trials of innovative thinkers (being regarded as highly eccentric) they elevated measurement to an all-embracing credo and firmly established it as one of the central tasks of management.

Their thinking still holds sway today and is variously called 'business analysis, industrial engineering, organization and methods and systems analysis. In the midst of modern day scorecards, dashboards and strategy maps we still look toward the basic measurement of performance described by Frank Gilbreth as a way to understand process size and effectiveness.

My Life and Work [3]
–Henry Ford

The measure of true leadership is turning theory into practice and Henry Ford quite simply took the ideas of Taylor and the Gilbreths to a new level of practical implementation. Brilliant in its simplicity Ford introduced a series of innovations and practical approached to revolutionizing the production of cars. Nearly a century ago the radical production line ideas completely changed a fledgling industry into a major piece of the industrials worlds economic jigsaw with reduced prices, extended operations (now known as supply chain management) and improvements to the article, in this case the Ford car.

Ford understood that price reduction on a large scale would stimulate demand, and through increased sales then costs in turn could be reduced. During the period of 1908 and 1916 he reduced prices by 60% at a time when demand was such that he could have easily raised them. Embracing the ideas of scientific management Ford realized that he could control the market through low prices, standardization and the focus on what customers really wanted. His drive to produce the then ubiquitous Model T set an example for the world to follow in improving productivity, enhancing customer delivery and providing his work force with the first $5 wage – then twice the average for the industry.

In turn, Ford brought another process based approach to bear in thinking of his market, product and customers on a global scale. Way ahead of his time, Ford thought of process activities flowing across functional and geographic boundaries and through his standardization efforts brought previously expensive products within the reach of the common man. In the later stages of his innovation and roll out of he glimpsed the future and included time based competition into his thinking and practice. "Time waste differs from material waste in that there can be no salvage," he wrote. Only recently have we seen work that builds on this thinking and allows us to move forward to the next level of process innovation through *The Real Time Enterprise* (Fingar, 2004).

Of course Taylor, Gilbreth and Ford have been superseded by many fine practitioners and writers however their original magic stays the same. They articulated the very nature of business processes and brought to life a set of thinking and theory that is only today attracting the complete attention of the world's most progressive organizations.

References

[1] Frederick Winslow Taylor, *The Principles of Scientific Management, Dover Pubns (January 1998 Edition)*

[2] Frank Gilbreth, Motion Study, *A Method for Increasing the Efficiency of the Workman*
[3] Henry Ford, *My Life and Work, New York, Doubleday, Page & Co, 1923*

Two

BPM: From Common Sense to Common Practice

By Roger Burlton

INTRODUCTION: *Roger Burlton, President of Process Renewal Group, gives us a broad perspective on BPM as he discusses where BPM's roots lie, how BPM has evolved, what BPM is really all about, the sweeping changes BPM will introduce and what companies must do to position themselves for success as the BPM movement continues to gain momentum.*

Business Process Management as an organizational regimen is very tricky to get your head around due to its multi-disciplined nature. Depending on who you talk to, it can be positioned as many things for many purposes and that is the heart of its misunderstanding and frequent sub-optimization. I intend to treat BPM's diversity and breadth as its strength when viewed from a standpoint other than that of a functional perspective or a single point of view. I also intend to convey the essence of BPM as being merely a natural way of both looking at enterprises and getting things done within an organizational context. In this chapter, I have deliberately de-emphasized the enabling technical aspects of BPM; that will be covered in other chapters. Handled well, BPM should be no more that the application of common sense to logical business problems and opportunities. My challenge will be to convey this in a way that ensures that such common sense will become common understanding and common practice.

Performance Challenges

In my book, *Business Process Management: Profiting from Process*, I emphasized the critical nature of assessing everything we do with a performance lens firmly in place. I also outlined a number of pressures and challenges affecting organizational performance. These still hold true today. All of the following are front and center when it comes to corporate challenges that BPM must acknowledge and deal with:

- Shrinking business cycles,
- Commoditization of products and services,
- Cost pressures,
- Knowledge-based services,
- e-business,
- Globalization,
- Consolidation,
- Extended value chains,
- External stakeholder power growth

A Simple Profit / Performance Model

Figure 1 shows a simple chart to illustrate the options we face in dealing with these pressures. The purpose for all organizations is to be effective and efficient as well as increasingly adaptable. Ultimately, they must strive to make the most of their resources given their strategic intent and the multiple demands on these resources. I will refer to this objective as to optimize profit for want of a more universal term. Management's job is to defend attacks upon and increase the area between the curves.

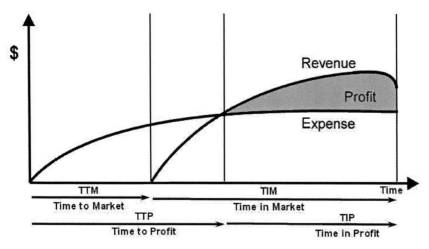

Figure 1: A Simple Process Performance Model

How is that possible? The first option is simple to identify, the reduction of the cost of running the business, which is easy to say and do until you take into account other factors and consider the requirement to sustain the organization beyond the short term. Shortening the time to market is on everyone's radar screen since the life of products and services in market is still shrinking in many industries. Elevating the return line requires the identification of the right offerings at the right time and great coordination in being ready to go to market on time on many fronts. Lastly, by anticipating and designing for impending changes in product and service characteristics and components you can lengthen the time in market through planned adaptability despite the fact that specific changes are indeterminate.

Everything you do organizationally or within a process needs to be assessed in these key performance terms. No organization is exempt. The question is how can this best be done? This chapter proposes a way of thinking and a way of managing that has been show to work based upon business processes as the synchronizer of 'what' work gets done and then 'how' work gets done. First, you have to change the way that organizations and managers collectively think about business processes.

Before the Industrial Revolution

Cleary, work with an intended result has been performed since the beginning of mankind. You can call this a process so what's really new?

Prior to the industrial revolution there were individuals and companies that delivered products and services to customers and consumers. Handcrafting of whole products was more the norm with a strong pride in workmanship and complete personal responsibility for results across instances of processes. The provision of whole and complete services from request or initiation to result was more the case than in the recent past. Scale-ability was not the big issue it can be today and resources became capable through apprenticeship towards a lifetime commitment to such a craft. There were many centuries of stability and changes occurred in an evolutionary manner. Today's definition of a Business Process, as set out in Figure 2, was not far off the mark.

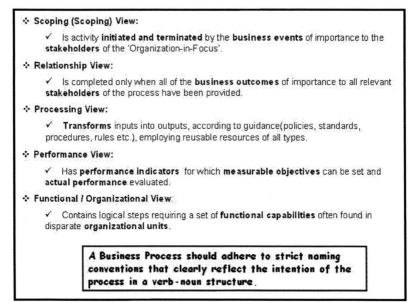

Figure 2: Business Process Definition

Consequences of the Industrial Revolution

With the advent of the Industrial Revolution, scale-ability requirements and the optimization of the scarce resources such as equipment and factories became a must to offset the high capital investments required for competitive advantage. Consequently, segmentation of work and the commoditization of the worker served to achieve the new reality. Work was still performed to produce outputs but workers were separated from overall results visibility; they just did their small job day-in and day-out. They were responsibility for compliance in repetitive work steps and lived in a command and control workplace. Given that products and services had long life cycles and most workers had low education levels, this model was suitable for the times.

A high degree of professional management was introduced after many decades and became the norm only after more than a century of transformation - not overnight, as it may seem from our distant backward perspective. Early in the 20th century, Frederick Taylor and others' Industrial Engineering approaches led to improvements in work steps and functions performed and the maturing of efficiency-oriented time and resource measurement systems for physical resource optimization and cost control.

These approaches were later supplemented by the Quality Management movement made popular by the likes of Deming, Juran and Crosby in the mid to later half of the century when products and services were still relatively stable. The drive was on for better, faster and cheaper ways of production. Of great importance, a breakthrough in thinking around quality occurred when its definition was recast in customer terms by these pioneers. For the first time in a long time processes were discussed in terms of how they supported the customers of the enterprise and the consumers of their offerings. This led the way for the externally-focused process improvement phase that followed next.

Business Process Re-engineering

There was great promise and hope that came when Michael Hammer coined the term 'Business Process Re-engineering' in 1990 in recognition of what many companies had done as a natural evolution beyond Total Quality Management. That period saw a rash of new management theories emerge which together provided a foundation for BPM today. Balanced Scorecard from Kaplan and Norton, Learning Organizations from Senge, Enterprise Architecture from Zachman are but a few of the concepts that have come together to provide a baseline for today's integrated thinking. However, BPR was the central tenet that exploded in popularity. It was also the reason for the near-demise of process thinking due to its common misunderstanding and poor application as well as some dogmatic ignorance of holistic organizational and cultural issues. Despite being cross-functional, BPR tended to emphasize transformation projects at the expense of sustainable structural multi-dimensional organizational change. Post projects, organizations often reverted to silo functional management structures with no ongoing nurturing of the resulting process asset. Due to the cost reduction orientation of its mandate, humans were typically ignored and jettisoned in many cases due to their high cost. Their knowledge was not seen as being central to ongoing sustainability and ultimately internal power struggles motivated by a legacy motivation model meant that benefits were often short lived, the solutions subverted and many companies put themselves at risk beyond the near term.

The Need for Integration

While many organizations were jumping on and off the BPR band-wagon, some were quietly applying a range of approaches that fused the best elements of many worlds and practices. They had learned that processes were the natural synchronizers or conductors of the business and that these processes were assets that had to be conceived, designed, developed and implemented as well as managed as is required for all assets. The management of holistic processes was almost like a trip back to the future wherein the best of the pre industrial revolution was being revived for today's world but for scaleable solutions for flexible products and services that allowed mass customization/personalization and rapid change as well as a strong customer orientation. Responsibility for process results became embedded structurally and measurements became more aligned with process stewardship with the commensurate account-abilities. Overall, business performance was starting to be tied to the business activity monitoring in near-real time. Now, the best practice organizations are using BPM in concert with or to make sense of the Balanced Scorecard, Customer Relationship Management, Enterprise Resource Planning, Enterprise Architecture, Six Sigma, Lean Thinking and Reference Frameworks such as the Supply Chain Operations Model (SCOR) as well as a myriad of other programs, techniques, technologies and management methods, all of which require the synchronizing capability that process management brings. Figure 3 shows my integration oriented definition of Business Process Management.

Managing BPM Itself

As I have noted already, Business Processes are themselves capabilities and as such must be managed as enterprise assets despite the fact you will not find them on the balance sheet. From a management perspective, this means planning investments in them, developing and improving them and governing their performance. In the days of BPR when processes were handled in isolation from one another, this oversight was not crucial corporately.

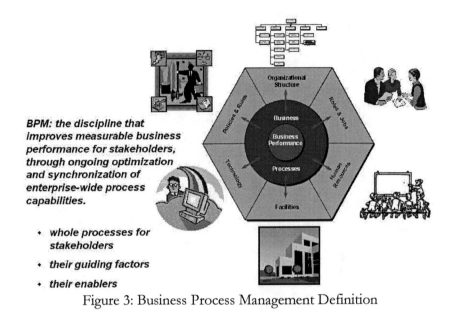

BPM: the discipline that improves measurable business performance for stakeholders, through ongoing optimization and synchronization of enterprise-wide process capabilities.

* *whole processes for stakeholders*
* *their guiding factors*
* *their enablers*

Figure 3: Business Process Management Definition

Now that organizations are looking at processes as a set of enterprise capabilities, they must deal with the whole set of processes for an organization together. As such, processes require governance just as financial, human and capital assets do. In every case, there is a requirement to remain true to outside requirements such as regulatory and stakeholder reporting, to be in synch with the strategic intent of the organization, to use resources wisely, to ensure accountability, to maintain alignment, to monitor and gate initiatives, and to consider opportunity costs corporately. Processes are no different. This requires an integrating framework that does all of this and a governance mechanism based on sound yet fundamentally different management principles.

Figure 4 shows a lifecycle process for process management itself. Its phases (clouds) and activities navigate the progression from the production of a company's business strategy through to the daily monitoring of results from its implemented strategic processes and reconnection to the front for renewal.

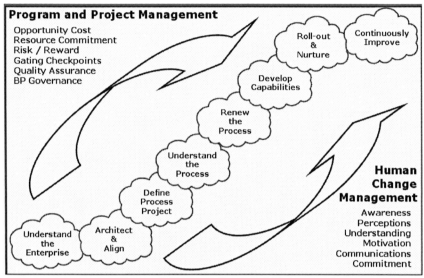

Figure 4: Process Renewal Framework

The Process Revolution and Evolution

As an Industrial Engineer with a keen interest in how people, organizations and societies change, I was somewhat surprised to discover that the Industrial Revolution was only so in comparison to historical timescales but not to human lifespan. Analysis of the move to industrialism that stared in the late 18th century in fact took more that a hundred years to accomplish. It was not an overnight phenomenon, as we may have believed. Changing businesses, companies, countries, society, culture and behavior is a multi-generational proposition. And it is clear that the Process Revolution that started in earnest sometime in the last half of the 20th century is indeed radical in nature but like its predecessor will likely evolve through a couple of more generations of managers and some corporate casualties along the way to become truly universal. The journey is, and will continue to be, painful. As in the Industrial Revolution, there will be incredible opportunities for those who embrace it whole heartedly to create new business models and to supplant the laggards who insist on hanging on to the past ways of working and managing. The evidence is apparent already for the early adopters.

The New Common Sense

So if true business process management is logical but so unconventional for many organizations today what would the new common sense logic look like? To answer this question, first let's examine how an ideal enterprise would appear to those on the outside with no visibility of its inner workings. There is no better place to start because outsiders only care about this perspective and they determine our success.

The External Perspective

The new enterprise is process-managed in order to stay in tune with its external business environment whether it likes the reality of it or not. It, first and foremost, recognizes that it must perform exceptionally well in all of its relationships and adjusts internally to do so rapidly and effectively. It knows what's happening or might happen in the outside world and does everything to anticipate and respond. That does not mean that it is not proactive and takes no risks. If appropriate it does. It manages at the stakeholder relationship level and organizes all its assets in alignment to this quest.

It continuously dispassionately asks:
- What is our business?
- What is the outside world like and what could it be like?
- Who are our stakeholders?
- What do they, and will they, care about?
- What products and services do we, and should we, offer?
- What else do we exchange with outsiders?
- What triggers our exchanges?
- What else do we have to know about our stakeholders?
- How can we evaluate and measure our performance?
- How well are we doing as far as stakeholders are concerned?
- How well are we doing as far as we are concerned?
- Are we positioned to continue to perform effectively?

- What has to change and by when?

All of these questions are about the external marketplace and those in it. The answers will become our criteria for managing internally. The new common sense demands an outside-in approach or as Steven Covey of the 'Seven Habits of Highly Effective People' may say "start with the end in mind." If you cannot answer these questions consistently across the management team of your corporation, then you are in for an uncomfortable ride.

The Internal Perspective

The challenge of the process-managed enterprise is to remain focused and capable to achieve the expectations of and the intentions towards the external environment that you have selected for yourself. This is the second tier of the new common sense. Now we have to identify, design, develop, implement and continuously manage new internal capabilities that are in synch with our ever-changing external criteria. Attributes of such enterprises include:

- Clear responsibility for external relationship management and performance (Relationship Custodians)
- Common definition of what are our start-to-end processes (Overall Process Map)
- Clear identification of which external stakeholders are involved with or affected by each process (Who cares?)
- Common understanding of what stakeholders expect and what we intend for them for each process (What do we want them to care about?)
- Understanding of what we exchange with them in this process and what triggers such exchanges?
- An organizational structure which supports process management as well as functional expertise
- Clear responsibility for all whole business processes that support the stakeholder relationships (Process Stewards)
- Processes built for the enterprise itself to look outward and deliver better intelligence for internal guidance and governance

- Processes that establish and communicate business strategy effectively.

- Processes that consider the various stages in the lifecycle of all stakeholder relationships

- An effective measurement and diagnostic system built for near real time evaluation and decision-making based on stakeholder and process performance.

- Information systems built to support full closed loop process execution from first trigger to last outcome of a stakeholder-initiated process(BPMS)

- Clarity on what has to change in each process and by when

- Capabilities (technological, human and physical asset) aligned with and managed by whole business processes.

- A set of business principles that support holistic thinking.

- Aligned incentives for all internal human resources and organizations to assure motivation to deliver against the outside requirements.

Once again, I would contend that, if you had just arrived on the planet from another galaxy, this is what you would expect to see if you thought that the human race cared enough and was capable about doing the right things right.

BPM as Common Practice

Continuing in the spirit of common sense, I will now address the issue of what we can do to realize the type of organization described so far. I will describe a logical structured method for working in a process oriented enterprise.

"Principles"

I am a great believer in principles to guide design, action and decision-making. No set of rules and procedures will ever be able to articulate every situation and nuance of possible action in a business process. You need something to fall back upon in reading a situation and doing what makes sense. The approach will follow some tried and true fundamentals that will guide you in circumstances whereby documented methods are insufficient and when you need to adjust from the exact documented steps. Some of the critical principles are as follows.

"Start with the end in mind"

When running an instance of a process or designing one the Stephen Covey advice is paramount. If it is not crystal clear to everyone as to what constitutes later success when the process is over and everything is done to add value to that vision you are sunk. The process results will be inconsistent, the stakeholders will be disappointed and the process will come under attack – both for the process execution and for its transformation. The simple message is that a clear and shared vision is required when you start. Do not leave home without it.

"Performance driven"

Every process, in order to be manageable, must be measurable and driven towards the attainment of agreed performance objectives. Finding performance metrics and setting targets is not so hard. Finding the right ones is very hard. As Norton and Kaplan of Balanced Scorecard fame have reported 'what you measure is what you get' so you better be sure that it is aligned with your and your stakeholders' process performance expectations. Performance attainment must become the basis for design, operational feedback, assessment and improvement of processes to cut through perceptions, resistance and internal politics. Without it, behavior will not change and the right results will not accrue.

"Stakeholder-driven"

Consistent with the prior two principles is the requirement for the absolute passionate commitment to and unwavering focus on the stakeholders of the process and their requirements. They are the only reason the process exists. Some will be active participants and others will be keenly interested and ultimately affected by what happens. The criteria for process performance must start and end with both their and your needs and desires. Trying to design and conduct processes without this perspective that serves as design criteria as the paramount consideration is delusional and at best sub-optimal.

"Criteria before decisions"

The root cause of most poor decisions in any business scenario and within all processes is that there is a lack of consistent criteria to guide action. Often decisions are made based on personal biases that vary based on the individual's experience, position or difference of opinion. Without shared and clear decision-making reference points that are carefully pre-considered, documented and communicated available to the decision makers, decisions will be inconsistent, easily challenged and not supported. Early process steps in every process must be built in to get acceptance of criteria to be applied in later ones.

"First things first"

Another Covey principle that must be strongly considered is the one that states that you have to start somewhere and that you may as well do what makes sense and sets the process off in the right direction. Failure to do this will undoubtedly result in errors, delays, rework, and downstream customer dissatisfaction. As mentioned before, the biggest cause of lack of process performance is what you did or did not do earlier in the process. So, after thoughtful design, trust the process and do all the steps and do not skip conducting good planning and preparation work or it will cost you later. When designing processes make sure your methodology has adequate consideration for whole process design not just the visible part at the end.

"Next things next"

Even if you get off on the right foot, either an irrational misdirected rush to get all changes implemented at once often takes over or the organizational power plays take off and blind all other logical considerations. The consequences can be devastating since the enterprise must live with them every day post transformation. The sequence is simple define who cares and what they care about, then products and service interactions, then define what gets done, then how it gets done, then the rules that govern the work, then the capabilities required in terms of technologies and human competencies, then where work will be done and then the organizational model required to do so. Throughout each of these, the human change communication and transformation must be managed. The mixing-up of this sequence is a major factor in the design and implementation dysfunction seen in business processes and the inappropriate set of technologies and other capabilities that are not aligned to process requirements and stakeholder needs and ultimately business performance. In brief:

- Design stakeholder relationships before processes
- Design processes before technological capabilities
- Design processes before human competencies

- Design processes and human competencies before organizations
- Design and execute the stakeholder communication program continuously

BPM Methodology Fundamentals

In order to realize the intent of the principles of BPM that works, significant architecture, analysis and design work must occur consistent with the principles previously addressed. Every component must contribute towards the establishment of a process-organized capability to deliver business performance and its improvement. The following Table 1 will describe the requirements of a methodology in terms of what we need to know, in what order, what tools we need to capture it and the way it contributes to business performance.

What Do We need to Know?	*What Management Tool will we use?*	*How will it Contribute to Business Performance*
What Organization are we optimizing?	"Organization-in-Focus" Scope Model	Business Definition
What are the external pressures and drivers that the organization must deal with?	Driver and Market Analysis	Business's Market Performance Assessment
What does the organization want to become and by when?	Business Strategic Intent Documentation	Strategic Objectives
What are the external stakeholders for the organization?	Stakeholder Map – Role Hierarchy	Stakeholder Relationship KPIs & Performance Objectives
What products and services do we exchange with our stakeholders?	Stakeholder Exchange / Interaction Map	Product and Service KPIs & Performance Objectives
What other items do we exchange with them?	Stakeholder Exchange / Interaction Map	Product and Service & Stakeholder Relationship KPIs & Performance Objectives
What must we do as an organization to meet our stakeholder intentions?	Process Architecture Map – levels 1 and 2	Aligned Process Goals, KPIs and Performance Objectives
How should we organize best to meet our process requirements?	Process Stewardship Map and Organization Chart	Process Organization KPIs & Performance Objectives
What technology resources must we have in place in order to perform what we must do?	Enterprise Technology Architecture Models	Technology Capability Goals and Performance Objectives
What human skills and competencies	Human Competencies	HR Goals and Perform-

do we need in order to perform what we must do?	Map	ance Objectives
How should we allocate our investment resources to achieve maximum performance?	Transformation Program Plan	Transformation Goals, KPIs & Program Performance Objectives
What is the actual performance of the 'Organization-in Focus'	Performance Monitoring Results	Actual Measures against above Objectives

Table 1

The table shows that there is a lot to know if you want to truly improve business performance through the organizing effect of business processes. It also shows that there are multiple models or maps that are required showing different aspects of the 'Organization in Focus' Like maps of a country that show political regions, precipitation, temperature or population, these performance-oriented maps are related and all are important. They answer the questions posed by different perspectives. They must be aligned by the process perspective in order to build a full performance management capability that is required for process managers to manage processes and outcomes. The Process Methodology for process management described earlier is designed to organize and integrate all of the requirements into a repeatable approach that can be trusted to deliver. The methodology described in my book as shown earlier in Figure 4 attempts to honor these principles and structure while dealing with the multiple perspectives required.

Summary

I have attempted to show that, despite the fact that processes have been with us for ever, we have a long way to go. The opportunity to exploit them, however, is still with us since many organizations are still largely dysfunctional when it comes to seamlessly doing the work required connecting to and from the outside stakeholder world. Their processes are not designed and managed holistically. Their methodologies are short sighted and partial. Many do not know what they do not know when embarking on a process venture. This chapter has provided the common sense for effective process management and the start for the establishment of some common practices to allow repeatable success in your enterprise.

Three

Operational Transformation: Get Ready for Extreme Competition

By Peter Fingar
(adapted from *The Real-Time Enterprise*, Meghan-Kiffer Press)

INTRODUCTION: *Just what really lies at the heart of business process management? What is it beyond today and where can it take us? Join Peter Fingar as he describes the Operational Transformation opportunity that BPM can lead to as part of an evolved business practice, resulting in an organization inherently geared to sustaining competitive advantage.*

KEY POINTS: *During the first fifty years of using computers in business, automation has been focused on record keeping. But, in case you hadn't noticed, that's changing, changing utterly. As we enter the second fifty years of business automation, computers are being deployed in a way that changes how companies do what they do, how they do their work, how they operate and conduct business. Rather than just speed up what companies already do, real-time computer-assisted business processes will bring about deep structural changes and make Operational Transformation the next frontier for gaining and sustaining competitive advantage.*

"Things have changed in a thousand small ways as a result of the Internet— email, online banking, information access, connections among business partners, online procurement... the list goes on. As the cumulative effect of the thousand points of light of today's business Internet reach the stage of total and immediate access, it becomes clear that a new kind of company, the company of the future, will emerge. In fact, it already has. It's the real-time enterprise." –Peter Fingar, MIT Lecture.

There is no doubt something new is going on in business, though it may not be clear exactly what. In the quest for the Next Big Thing in business, you are probably convinced by now that the next big thing isn't about technology. The technology spending craze of the second half of the 1990s is proof enough. You also know that the search for new productivity and adaptability must center on squeezing out costs while at the same time finding new ways to get closer to your never-satisfied customers whose needs have also greatly changed under the current economic realities. You know you need to look beyond the walls of your company to seek new operational innovations and to sense and respond to new market opportunities. You know you must become more proactive and less reactive to change.

Yet, although many business people have said, "I told you so, the Internet was only a fad whose bubble burst in the dot-com meltdown," you know the Internet has only begun to transform business. You rightly suspect that the anywhere, anytime, anything connectivity of the Internet can enable unprecedented opportunities for innovation and competitive advantage.

But any plans for business reinvigoration will call for information system capabilities that currently do not exist. You may be responsible for creating these capabilities within your organization. The tools at your disposal include current systems, infrastructure, staff and practices. Each of these represents a significant investment and currently provides value. But they are just not up to the task at hand. You know you need more, but more of what? You know all the latest management innovations such as lean manufacturing and Six Sigma. But those methods only help you perfect what you already do in your business, and you know you need to do something new, something you are not already doing, to gain new business advantage.

Again, you reflect on the universal connectivity of the Internet in thinking about the Next Big Thing. There are numerous advanced technologies and techniques that could help you harness the Internet, but which ones? How will they enable you to transform your business? How can they create new sources of competitive advantage? How do you implement them while leveraging your current investments and business practices?

Of course you are still wary of the Internet, for as the millennium clock rolled over to the 21st century, that something new was thought to be the dot-com revolution, where everything business people knew was wrong, for the Internet had supposedly changed the very rules of business. Traditional business fundamentals were thrown out in favor of stratospheric initial public offerings of firms established by twenty-something year old entrepreneurs.

Indeed the Internet had worked magic on public markets and there seemed no end in sight. That is, until the dot-com crash of 2000, where over an 18-month period the sucking sound could be heard when almost three and a half trillion dollars evaporated as financial markets imploded. Many thereafter concluded that the Internet fad was over. Others, like GE's legendary CEO, Jack Welch, concluded that the impact of the Internet on business had just begun, for the Internet wasn't about a Web site or an IPO, it was all about a major business transformation—Operational Transformation. That transformation has just begun and has been heralded by two predominate buzzwords, the *real-time enterprise (RTE)* and *business process management (BPM)*. A businessperson would have to have his or her head in the sand not to have seen these terms in the business press these days. There's lots of hype. But under the hype curves of these new three-letter acronyms a whole new world of gaining and sustaining competitive advantage is unfolding.

The impact of the Internet's universal connectivity doesn't mean a change in *what* goods and services a company provides, nor does it mean the invention of new industries. Those stories belong to the invention of the steam engine, electricity, railroads and other icons that ushered in the Industrial Age. Instead, universal connectivity signals a change in *how* companies deliver their goods and services—that is, how they do what they do, how they and their trading partners accomplish their work; that's what I call *Operational Transformation*. It's about *how work gets done*, and though that may sound a little boring, Operational Transformation is the next frontier of business advantage.

Today, ingrained work patterns linger from traditional business designs that originated with Adam Smith's concepts of specialization and division of labor in the 1776 book, *The Wealth of Nations*. But change companies must, or their competitors who reinvent the way they work will run circles around them. What GE, Wal-Mart, Virgin Group, Toyota, JetBlue, Dell Computer and other often-cited pioneers have done is *change the game in their industries by making deep structural changes, that, in turn, have been made possible by Internet-enabled business process innovation*—they reinvented the very ways they operate their businesses.

Forrester's CEO, George Colony explained the need for Operational Transformation against the backdrop of the universal connectivity of the Internet; "Whether it's the stirrup, the PC, or electricity, technology has always required change in the way humans work. You don't farm the same way with a hoe as you do with a plow. General Motors didn't organize its robotically driven Saturn production line the way Rolls-Royce structured its hand-built assembly process." You don't conduct business the same way with faxes, phone calls, meetings and emails as you do with real-time business processes delivered over the Internet.

Further, Internet-enabled business process innovations are not one-time events. It's the "pace of innovation" that counts in today's global, and often dog-eat-dog, business world. Michael Dell, who has made his fortune by selling commoditized IT products and services, believes a given business process innovation is not the endgame; it's the starting line. As Andrew Park reported in *Business Week*, "Sure, Dell is the master at selling direct, bypassing middlemen to deliver PCs cheaper than any of its rivals. And few would quarrel that it's the model of efficiency, with a far-flung supply chain knitted together so tightly that it's like one electrical wire, humming 24/7. Yet all this has been true for more than a decade. And although the entire computer industry has tried to replicate Dell's tactics, none can hold a candle to the company's results. Today, Dell's stock is valued at a price-earnings multiple of 40, loftier than IBM, Microsoft, Wal-Mart Stores, or General Electric."

"As it turns out, it's how Michael Dell manages the company that has elevated it far above its sell-direct business model. What's Dell's secret? At its heart is his belief that the status quo is never good enough, even if it means painful changes for the man with his name on the door. When success is achieved, it's greeted with five seconds of praise followed by five hours of postmortem on what could have been done better. Says Michael Dell: 'Celebrate for a nanosecond. Then move on.' After the outfit opened its first Asian factory, in Malaysia, the CEO sent the manager heading the job one of his old running shoes to congratulate him. The message: This is only the first step in a marathon."[1]

Welcome to 21st century business, where the winners are agile, mobile and play hardball. They operate their game-changing business processes in real time, following each business innovation with a marathon of process improvement and optimization. They harness the humble, yet mighty, *business process* to form global value-delivery systems that provide comprehensive computer-assisted support, from their customers' customers to their suppliers' suppliers, squeezing out both *costs* and *time* throughout a business web of players interconnected by the Internet. They operate 24/7, not only providing customers, employees and suppliers with real time, actionable information. They provide *self-service* operations so that all involved can actually *conduct business*, anywhere, anytime—they can do more than just see actionable information, they can *act* on it. The company, its suppliers and its customers are all employed by the same value-delivery system—they are fused together as one—each playing its part in creating, delivering and consuming economic goods and services. Indeed, Operational Transformation is the next source of competitive advantage, and companies that pursue this new mode of business will become the process-managed, real-time enterprises that prosper in the decade ahead.

Operational Transformation and Extreme Competition

Years ago, Dr. Michael Porter, Harvard Business School's authority on competition and strategy, concluded that, "Activities, then, are the basics of competitive advantage. Overall advantage or disadvantage results from all a company's activities. The essence of strategy is choosing to perform activities differently than rivals do." But it's not so easy to change the activities a company currently performs, even if these are now dysfunctional work patterns, for ingrained work habits are hard to break. Even with the universal connectivity of the Internet, many companies still operate in the same basic ways they have always operated, coordinating work manually, conducting meetings, shuffling paper and making repeated phone calls to correct even the simplest of errors in day-to-day business transactions.

Meanwhile, others, some of which are highlighted in this book, actually conduct business with real-time business processes that reach across the globe. Using the principles of business process management, they have made deep structural changes in their organizations that make them different. They are *time-based competitors* and are swift to make major course corrections, while delighting their customers day in and day out with *responsiveness*, rolling out innovations with regularity. It's all in how they do what they do, and they clearly have reinvented how they do what they do. They are preparing for a new form of global, *extreme competition.*

Operational Transformation requires looking outside the walls of a given company and managing the complete value-delivery system, from its customers' customers, to its suppliers' suppliers. While the Internet provides the digital nervous system for the 21st century company, a new category of business process management software provides what's needed to harness that universal connectivity for business advantage. Companies that master real-time business process management can:

- Automate the Primary Activities of the Firm.
- Radically Reduce the Cost of Business Interactions.
- Provide Self-Service That Delights, While Cutting Costs.
- Radically Reduce the Cost of Software While Speeding Up its Development Time.
- Execute on Innovation with Great Speed and Agility.
- Sense and Respond to Demand.
- Make Deep Structural Adjustments.
- Offer Product Services.

Automate the Primary Activities of the Firm. Michael Porter's work on competitive advantage separates a firm's primary activities that deliver value to customers, from its support activities that represent the overhead of being in business (paying the rent, paying employees, human resource management and so on). Primary activities are about innovation, sales and marketing, and customer support—all the rest, the support activities, are essentially back-office costs.

During the first fifty years of business automation, rarely were the firm's primary activities the object of automation, for software had not matured to the point where it could address the complex and oft-changing primary activities of the company. The new category of business process management systems changes that. For example, through its Digitization Initiative, GE is intent on reallocating its resources, reducing the back-office to 10% of resource expenditures, with all the rest devoted to its primary activities. In short, for companies that master real-time process management, business automation will, for the first time, bear directly on the *money-making aspects* of the business instead of the *bean counting*. Because it is the uniqueness of a firm's primary activities that distinguish it from competitors, computer-assistance will give companies the tools they need to differentiate by performing their activities in unique ways—the essence of Porter's notion of strategy.

Radically Reduce the Cost of Business Interactions. It's the cumulative costs across the entire value chain that customers see, and those costs are driven as much by information costs as they are in the actual delivery of goods or services. By pushing down information costs of the entire value-delivery system, companies such as Dell have established dominance in their industries. Time is the critical variable in squeezing out costs, for *squeezing out time* can reduce costs such as inventory, overproduction and transaction handling costs. Reducing or eliminating information lag time across the value chain has a positive impact on the bottom lines of all value-chain participants, including customers. Long ago, management luminary, Peter Drucker, observed that it's the new entrant in an industry that reduces overall costs—both direct and indirect—by managing the entire economic chain that comes to dominate. Companies that master Internet-enabled business process management can gain a new capability for managing costs across the entire value-delivery system.

Provide Self-Service That Delights, While Cutting Costs. Advanced techniques of delivering self-service via the Internet can cut costs of customer care significantly because the customer no longer requires a service representative to handle most service-related issues. A new generation of *process-powered* self-service can increase customer loyalty because response times to problems can be significantly reduced—no more multiple and frustrating visits to touch-tone hell at the call center to solve even the most straightforward request. This new generation of computer-assisted self-service goes well beyond the simple tasks like checking an account balance or transferring funds from one account to another. Process-powered self-service capabilities provide a collaboration environment so that customers can have a *dialog* with a company to solve issues that were not anticipated and built into so-called Help menus and frequently asked questions and other already-common self-service techniques.

This new generation of self-service software is increasingly capable of becoming a company's Concierge. Smart companies, such as Progressive Insurance, are making their customers as smart as they are by providing quotes from their competitors. Its Concierge knows its customers will check anyway, so it provides a complete service and does the leg work for them, creating trust in the company. Progressive knows that *trust is the foundation for building lasting relationships* with customers and increasing their lifetime value to the company.

The relationship between a company and its customers doesn't end when a good or service is sold; that relationship has just begun, and must continue throughout the consumption of the good or service. Customer care activities are the most significant touch points with customers, for the cost of acquiring new customers is ten times that of selling to an existing, happy, customer. On the other hand, a dissatisfied customer will tell nine others about his or her experience with a company. Indeed, self-service can provide the *double-leverage* of cutting costs while increasing satisfaction. This represents a truly new source of competitive advantage, for it's a sure formula for strengthening customer relationships. As writer Kevin Kelly noted, "The central economic imperative of the Industrial Age was to increase productivity. The central economic imperative of the network economy is to amplify relationships."[2]

Karen Rogers, VP of FedEx.com, gives a sampling of FedEx's ever-growing self-service functionality, "You can locate a FedEx station, get signature proof of delivery, request a courier for pickup, download global trade tools, get forms for shipping international packages, estimate duties and taxes, request invoice adjustments, and connect to the customer service organization."[3]

"Other self-service Web apps include FedExShip Manager, which lets customers centrally manage domestic and international shipping; Global Trade Manager, which helps users estimate duties and taxes on international shipments; and a tool called Alive that lets customers manage and track ground and freight shipments from Asia to the United States. Technology-based innovations—whether new wrist-mounted bar-code scanners for on-the-go workers or the ability to know the contents of incoming packages provided by FedEx's InSight application—are viewed within FedEx as ways to differentiate the company's products and services."

"Only one factor is rated more critical than innovation to the IT team's mission. 'We will differentiate on innovation,' Dottie Berry, a FedEx V.P. says. 'We will dominate on speed.'"[4]

Radically Reduce the Cost of Software While Speeding Up Development Time. The notion of delivering "software as a service" is all the rage in the technology world. Software components are rendered as *services* delivered over the Web. In short, *Web services provide the foundation for a programmable Internet.* Such Web services commoditize common automation tasks, driving down the costs, and making it child's play to combine two or more components for a higher-level purpose (e.g., combining catalog software, with a shopping cart and credit processing to sell goods on the Web).

Just about any form of software can be delivered as a Web service, and, while the software components themselves become commoditized, their combinations become the opposite of a commodity. The situation is like the commodity, the alphabet. Although everyone has access to the alphabet, only those with creativity and skill are able to fashion unique and high-value works of literature. Although everyone has access to Web services, only those with creativity and skill will be able to fashion unique and high-value business processes. That's where business process management software comes in, for it provides the capabilities needed to orchestrate and choreograph Web services into *unique* end-to-end processes that deliver distinctive value to customers.

While Web services commoditize software—and industry *best practices*—business process management software is the secret sauce that can blend software components to let companies perform their activities in infinitely different ways than their rivals—again, the essence of Porter's notion of competitive advantage is to be different. Likewise, industry best practices can be bundled, unbundled and rebundled in unique ways to create innovation practices—*innovation practices* supersede commoditized *best practices* as the way to escape the commoditization trap. That often means harvesting the best practices from different industries for business advantage.

BPMG (bpmg.org) council member, Mark McGregor, describes how best practices can be drawn from several industries to create what he calls *next practices*, "What if you looked to brand-based companies such as Coca Cola for your ideas on marketing, what if you looked at someone like Amazon for your inspiration in building on-line shops for your products and possibly someone like McKinsey as your inspiration for providing service? I am sure you will agree that a company that delivered products to the same quality as a pharmaceutical company and services to the standard of McKinsey, while being as smart at brand awareness as Coca Cola and as easy to buy from as Amazon—would cause more than a few ripples in its marketplace."[5]

Execute on Innovation with Great Speed and Agility. Business innovation is no longer a discrete event; it's now the "pace of innovation" that counts. It's never been easy to transform innovative ideas into action, and ultimately, all innovations can be copied. On the other hand, by the time competitors catch up to the innovators or fast followers, the innovators have pushed the envelope once again, running circles around their competitors. Time and time again, innovations from companies like Toyota, Amazon and Dell are there for all to see, but deep structural changes and other trade-offs make it difficult to imitate or replicate the innovator. Rather than try to catch up with Toyota, in 2004 Ford licensed Toyota's hybrid engine. Rather than try to catch up with Amazon, Borders Books outsourced its entire online operation to Amazon.

Business innovation is no longer an episodic, one-time event; it's the launching pad for a stream of follow-on innovations, and savvy innovators use real-time business process management to *execute on innovation* and to gain the agility they need to increase the velocity of innovation. They set the pace of innovation to stay ahead of the competition. *The ability to execute on innovation is at least as important as the innovation itself,* and in today's technology-dependent business environment the bond between innovation and execution can only be sealed with real-time business process management.

Sense and Respond to Demand. Wal-Mart is notorious for many of its hardball business tactics, but one of the more surprising aspects of this 800-pound industry gorilla is its willingness to share demand information in real time with its suppliers and their suppliers. This willingness isn't to be mistaken for an act of altruism; it's an act of business acumen.

By beaming demand signals in real time to all its suppliers, Wal-Mart enables the entire value chain to respond to actual demand, rather than to forecast. Forecasts, by definition, are wrong. It's this information chain on steroids that allows products to flow from manufacturer to consumer without being unduly imprisoned in Wal-Mart warehouses. The *make-to-demand* business model of the real-time enterprise is a source of competitive advantage that supersedes the forecast-buy-sell model, the supply-push model of the past, with a radically streamlined demand-pull model of business.

Make Deep Structural Adjustments. The shift from supply-push to demand-pull as a business strategy applies to almost all industries, but *it requires structural changes in organizations and their cultures.* In other words, Operational Transformation is much more than automation or digitizing business processes. Becoming a process-managed real-time enterprise requires that companies adopt new business models which, in turn, require organizational realignment and changes in *mental models* of the people that make up the organization. In the past, people and cultural issues were kept at bay because companies did not have the technological infrastructures for making either rapid or deep structural change. But now, with the advent of the Internet and business process management software, they do. As a result, people and cultural issues have surfaced as *the* critical factors of change.

Business process change and innovation is one side of a two-sided coin. Deep structural adjustments to organizations is the other. Companies that can tightly interlock strategy and organizational alignment to Internet-enabled business process innovation will be able to cross a cultural chasm that others cannot. To address this issue, GE has begun training its senior executives in innovation management, for innovation isn't just some nifty business concept; it demands changes in the very ways of doing business if it's to bring about new sources of competitive advantage. The big challenges are cultural and organizational changes, and these *monumental* challenges must be addressed as such.

Offer Product Services. Because consumers want solutions, not products (they really want a hole, not a drill), smart companies have transformed from just selling products to selling product services. General Motors no longer just sells cars; it sells *a safer, easier and more productive ride* with its OnStar technology and services. GE has grown from a product-based company into a services company that also makes great products. Seventy percent of GE's revenue comes from services and, increasingly, from product services. Two decades ago, when Jack Welch took the helm, only 15 percent of GE's revenues came from services. Welch noted in a 2001 shareholder's meeting that product service at GE today is as high-technology as anything the firm does.[6] Smart companies are embedding information and information services into their products, e.g., telephones are becoming Web browsers. But, as strategic business futurist, Dr. More, notes, that's just the beginning of some already deployed technologies with a much larger future ahead; a future where companies will sell product services and *smart* products.

Getting There

For technologists and other BPM insiders, business process management is all the rage these days. But business leaders have grown weary of three-letter acronyms—they want results. What can BPM actually do for them? As long as the BPM conversation is restricted to technologists and Six Sigmists, it's likely to become just another technique for squeezing out costs and making incremental performance improvements. On the other hand, for some early pioneers where the conversation has reached the board room, BPM portends much more, as we have discussed in this chapter.

Indeed, there is a Next Big Thing in business, but it's not just about technology and incremental improvement; it's about *operational transformation,* driven by the emergence of a wired, flat world. It's about the fusion of business operations and information technology to the point of unity. It's about forging brand new end-to-end business processes that cross the entire multi-company value delivery system—where no managed business process has gone before. It's about value-chain business process management (VC-BPM) overarching enterprise business process management (EBPM). This epic transformation is well under way, and is on a scale that can only be called *the great 21st century business reformation,* where 20th century business doctrines, dogmas and practices are being called into question. Is your company ready for extreme competition?

References.

[1] Park, Andrew, "What You Don't Know About Dell," Business Week, November 23, 2003.

[2] Kelly, Kevin, *New Rules for the New Economy: 10 Radical Strategies for a Connected World,* Penguin Books, 1999.

[3] http://www.line56.com/print/default.asp?ArticleID=4110

[4] http://www.informationweek.com/story/showArticle.jhtml?articleID=17300234

[5] http://www.bpmg.org/articles.php

[6] Chairman Jack Welch's remarks at the firm's annual shareowners meeting in Atlanta, GA, April 25, 2001.

Four

Strategy and BPM

By Andrew Spanyi

INTRODUCTION: *This chapter by Andrew Spanyi, Executive Coach with The Business Process Management Group, presents the case for Strategy and BPM, adapted from his book Business Process Management is a Team Sport – Play it to Win!*

"No sensible decision can be made any longer without taking into account not only the world as it is, but the world as it will be."
–Isaac Asimov

It is now generally accepted that business process improvement is one of the important tools in an organization's tool kit for reducing costs and improving the quality of products and services offered to customers. What is less well known, and even less frequently practiced, is that the application of business process management principles can empower firms to make tough strategic choices and better engage the entire organization in the execution of strategy.

Yet there is ample evidence that a customer focused, business process approach applies to both the formulation and implementation of strategy. As far back as 1996, strategy guru Michael Porter emphasized that "Activities, then, are the basics of competitive advantage." He made a compelling argument that overall advantage or disadvantage results from the integrated design of all of a company's activities, not only a few, and then went on to say that "The essence of strategy is choosing to perform activities differently than rivals do." [1]

Gary Hamel, another leading name in the field of strategy, stressed in his book *Leading the Revolution* that most companies who wish to redesign their business models must first challenge leadership's dominant mental models by asking and answering some key questions including: [2]

- What is the basis for differentiation?
- What core competencies are important?
- What core processes are critical?

Alan Brache, the author of *How Organizations Work*, was one of the early thought leaders in process thinking and an executive in Kepner-Tregoe's strategy practice. He repeatedly called attention to the fact that the formulation and implementation of a firm's strategy relies significantly on the definition, improvement and management of its critical business processes. [3]

Given all this evidence from thought leaders in both academia and consulting firms, why is it that more firms do not practice business process thinking and acting in formulating and implementing their strategy? Why aren't more companies jumping on the business process management bandwagon? Don't they understand that a firm's strategy can only be executed by improving and managing its enterprise business process?

As Hamel intimated, a large part of the answer is to be found in the dominant and very traditional mental models practiced by many leaders today.

Unfortunately, far too many of today's business leaders still cling to a traditional functional mindset where they continue to see their business as a collection of functions on the organization chart. They have not evolved their thinking to a more adaptive paradigm where it's the performance of the enterprise's business processes – and not departmental performance - which creates value for customers. This traditional way of thinking is indeed problematic. It produces a set of beliefs and behaviors which collectively work to sub-optimize organizational performance. Specifically, the traditional functional mindset promotes:

- Silo behaviour and Turf protection
- An undue preoccupation with organization structure
- A distorted view of performance measurement and executive rewards
- A continuation of 'command and control' management practices

It is this traditional way of thinking that leads firms to launch dozens, and even hundreds, of unconnected, un-integrated, and often overlapping improvement initiatives. This is one of the major causes many firms fail to make tough strategic choices.

For those firms who recognize the limitation of traditional functional thinking - there is good news! The adoption of business process management principles and practices can be instrumental in facilitating not only clarity of strategic direction, but also aid in establishing flawless execution, a robust culture and an enabling structure.

The key to successful leadership today is influence, not authority.
–Kenneth Blanchard

Stated differently, in the absence of deploying BPM principles and practices at the enterprise level, firms find it more difficult to make tough strategic choices and consequently, the results from many improvement efforts are likely to be sub-optimized.

What are these essential BPM principles? A summary of the first five principles most relevant to this topic is offered below, and a full treatment is available in this author's book: *Business Process Management is a Team Sport: Play It to Win!* [4]

The first essential principle is to look at the business from the outside-in, from the customer's perspective, as well as the inside-out. Why? To be successful, companies must explicitly understand and measure what customers require and the extent to which current business process performance meets customer and company requirements. The key steps involve first expressing customer requirements, typically in terms of value, quality and timeliness. Next, explicitly define the enterprise business processes to gain clarity around the inputs, outputs, major sub-steps, and functions involved for each. Then, establish the performance measures for those processes and assess current business process performance in terms of both a customer and a company point of view. This results in a draft enterprise business process model.

The second essential principle states that the company's strategy needs to be tightly integrated with its enterprise business processes. Why? The simple undeniable truth is that work gets done through cross-functional business processes. So articulating strategy in business process terms facilitates both implementation and communication. Most organizations find that business process thinking helps articulate strategic initiatives in plain language, with measurable results. The key steps involved here include assessing the gap between current and desired performance in business process terms, and developing a business process management plan which clearly indicates the ownership of the enterprise-level business processes and the degree of improvement for each business process.

The third principle is to articulate the firm's strategy such that it inspires, from the boardroom to the lunchroom, and remains front and center throughout the year. Why do this? Implementing strategy requires that people be on the same page in terms of what needs to be done. This involves linking vision and mission to key strategic initiatives expressed in business process terms, such that people can relate their individual efforts in making strategy happen. The main output of these activities is a communication plan.

The fourth principle is the launching pad for organizational alignment. It states that action needs to be taken to assure that the organization's core business processes are designed to deliver on its strategic goals. Again, work gets done via business processes. The key steps include a mid-level analysis to flesh out and validate the scope of work indicated by the business process management plan.

The fifth principle says that the organization design must enable business process execution. In this context, organization design is defined as the composite of structure, measures and rewards. Putting this into practice relies upon an iterative method linked to business process improvement activities.

In practical terms, the application of these essential principles to the effective formulation and implementation of strategy is outlined in Table 1 below.

Seems straightforward – doesn't it? So why is it that even those firms with a strong track record of business process improvement experience struggle in adopting this type of behavior?

Nothing is more desirable than to be released from an affliction, but nothing is more frightening than to be divested of a crutch.
–James Baldwin

STEP	ACTIVITY	DELIVERABLE
1	Define the Enterprise Wide Business Processes	An enterprise business process relationship map
2	Determine the Appropriate Business Process Measures	A set of the critical few metrics from both a customer and a company perspective expressed typically in terms of value, cost, quality, productivity and timeliness.
3	Determine current performance for the critical business processes.	Data on current performance for these key metrics.
4	Express the firm's strategy in business process terms	Statements that indicate which business processes need to be improved by how much to achieve strategic objectives.
5	Determine the size of the performance gap and determine priorities	A draft business process improvement and management plan.
6	Assign Business Process Owners and align Business Process Owner Rewards	Accountability for results of planned improvement and management efforts.
7	Develop and Communicate a Business Process Improvement and Management Plan	A vehicle for communicating and monitoring the implementation of the plan.

Table 1

There are a number of obstacles. The first is tradition, or in other words, we've always done it this way. To test this out, consider whether the following scenario applies to your organization. When the time comes for a company to develop its strategic plan, the leadership team, frequently in the company of a highly paid consultant, goes away on a "strategic retreat." There they debate and discuss all the typical questions which traditionally need to be answered to formulate strategy. These will include questions such as: What are our fundamental values/beliefs? What products and/or services will we offer? What customer groups will we serve? What will propel our growth? What will cause us to succeed? What financial and non-financial results will we achieve? What strategic initiatives must we do well at?

With a feeling of satisfaction, the leadership team returns to the day-to-day task of running the business, and staff prepares a binder with the key findings and plans from the strategic retreat. A few weeks later, the binder is complete and the leadership team assigns accountability for the strategic initiatives to department heads. Then what happens? Well, that depends. Sometimes progress is made, and sometimes not. But it's really not that important since the firm doesn't look at this material until just before their next strategic retreat. Sound familiar? That is why it takes a deliberate, conscious and collaborate leadership effort to change the way in which strategy is formulated and implemented.

The second obstacle is also related to tradition, but has more to do with a functional view of business. This is encountered by some firms who attempt to express strategy in business process terms. To appreciate the obstacle in question, just examine how a major chemical company expressed its enterprise processes in the schematic below.

A Major Chemical Company

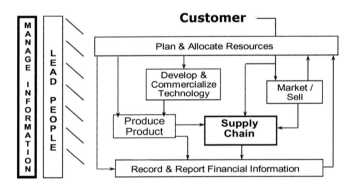

Can you see the problem or problems? If you said that this organization has defined their enterprise business processes mainly in the context of their functional departments, you are absolutely right.

Of course, simply renaming functional departments and calling them business processes doesn't magically make it so. It's not going to do much to help people better view the flow of value added work needed to create value for customers and shareholders.

There are some other issues as well, such as the lack of clarity on the inputs to and the outputs from these enterprise processes and lack of clarity around the critical few measures of performance.

The next schematic represents the efforts of the leadership team at a major IT services company to depict their enterprise business processes in the form of a one page view.

A Leader in Consulting and IT Services

Here we see an appreciation of the core business processes from an outside-in perspective. However, the enabling business processes are still represented in largely a functional context. What is interesting is that this firm uses internal "service level agreements" [SLA's] in an effort to assure that the so-called "shared services" provide the needed enablers to the core processes. While this is now moving in the right direction, there may still not be sufficient detail around the interdependence between the critical business processes to assure that the leadership team develops a shared understanding of which business processes need to be improved by how much to achieve strategic objectives.

The third obstacle is related to the challenge of focus. Most firms have launched far more projects than they can successfully execute. They lack focus on the critical few priorities which make a significant difference in organizational performance. Many of these projects take on a life of their own, consuming valuable resources, and the leadership team therefore needs to act deliberately and collaboratively to shut down the non-critical initiatives. That's often easier said than done.

The fourth obstacle relates to the difficulty of aligning recognition and reward systems with what is needed to enable business ownership. The old adage applies here "What gets measured gets done and what gets rewarded gets done consistently." If firms are truly intent on promoting a customer focused, business process view of the enterprise then it is necessary to both appoint process owners or stewards for the large business processes and reward these leaders for improving and managing these processes.

While these obstacles are daunting, they are by no means insurmountable. Those firms who take the genuine effort to define their enterprise business processes from a customer's point of view, assess current performance, and set desired performance, pass the first hurdle. Then they will be equipped to ask and answer the question: "Which of our business processes need to be improved by how much for us to reach our strategic objectives?" The answer to this question drives strategic focus and the development of an enterprise process improvement and management plan which creates the means to convert intention to action as implied in Table 1 above.

Expressing strategy in business process terms can be a powerful and inspirational way of keeping strategy front and center in people's minds and hearts throughout the year. This is because people identify more clearly with what needs to be done to improve the flow of work to create value for customers than with fuzzy, general statements of strategic direction. How to do it? By taking action to:

- Find multiple ways, using multiple media to communicate your core strategy and key messages on which business processes need to be improved by how much to reach strategic objectives

- Communicate a set of measures on how well you are delivering against customers' needs relative to the industry average and your key competitors

- Develop and implement a set of visible and significant rewards for those who significantly improve the company's ability to deliver on customer needs through observable, measurable improvement of the firm's critical business processes

Of course, that's only the beginning. In the final analysis, an organization will only achieve the flawless execution it seeks if the entire organization is engaged in executing strategy. That requires alignment of the firm's resources and concurrently shaping the firm's culture to move towards a fact based model.

Failing organizations are usually over-managed and under-led.
– Warren G. Bennis

Engaging the organization in executing strategy is largely a matter of leadership. It's not just about process in the traditional sense, where process is defined as a set of activities which convert an input into a value added output. Process is better defined as "how work is accomplished" – and that is why people matter enormously! After all, it's people who get things done in any organization.

That is precisely why leaders need to go beyond establishing strategic focus and also deliberately and collaboratively work to shape the culture of the organization by:

- Establishing a sense of urgency for key initiatives
- Following up
- Encouraging process and product innovation such that success is rewarded and failure is not fatal.
- Assuring that technology investment decisions are made such that the deployment of technology is first and foremost designed to enable the performance of people in executing key business processes
- Constantly investing in training to install a common language, and provide the necessary skills

If this seems to you to call for significant effort, you're right. It does. As Arthur Brisbane, the American journalist said, "The dictionary is the only place where success comes before work."

As some experts have pointed out, in up to 70% of cases, the challenge is not simply by formulating a strategy. Instead, it is by not getting things done, nor delivering on its commitments. The critical elements in engaging a broad cross-section of the organization on executing strategy requires sensitivity to both sequence and continuity and that is where business process thinking makes a critical difference.

Which are the key elements? There are several:

- Clearly articulating strategy
- Selecting the critical few measures of performance
- Assuring that roles and accountabilities are clear
- Aligning rewards and recognitions.
- Pulling it all together to shift organization culture.

Interested in assessing how you're doing? Then, take the following quiz:

1. To what extent does the leadership team see the business from the *outside-in* as well as the *inside-out*?

2. Have you developed a core strategy that is tightly integrated with the definition, management, and improvement of the enterprise's business processes such that there's a shared understanding as to which business processes need to be improved by how much to achieve strategic objectives?

3. Have you developed and communicated an enterprise business process improvement and management plan to assure that the organization's core business processes are designed to deliver on its strategic goals?

4. Have you taken a deliberate effort to articulate the firm's strategy such that it *inspires,* from the boardroom to the lunchroom, and remains front and center throughout the year?

5. Have you documented and communicated the links/interdependencies among the critical enterprise processes?

6. Has there been a deliberate effort to ensure that the organization design, as defined by the structure, measures, and rewards, enables effective business process execution?

7. Is there broad based agreement that the assessment and deployment of enabling technology needs to be based on the value added through enhanced business process performance?

8. Is the enterprise-wide performance measurement system "hard-wired" to budgets and operating reviews?

9. How well have you expressed both the financial and non-financial business process goals which define the strategic success of your enterprise?

10. How fluid is the top-down and bottom-up flow of information on progress towards achieving your strategic objectives?

11. Have you assured that each department's roles and incentives reflect the contributions it should make to each critical enterprise business processes?

12. How well do you share "lessons learned" across business units and geographic units, and is there clarity on the degree to which each business unit benefits from its relationships with other business units?

Is it worth the effort? Should you invest in the effort to apply business process management principles to make tough strategic choices and better engage your organization in the execution of strategy? You be the judge.

Make things as simple as possible - but no simpler.
—Albert Einstein

References.

---

[1] Porter, Michael, "What is Strategy?" *Harvard Business Review*, November-December 1996, pgs 61-78

[2] Hamel, Gary, *Leading the Revolution*, Harvard Business School Press, 2000

[3] Brache, Alan, *How Organizations Work*, Wiley, 2002

[4] Spanyi, Andrew, *Business Process Management is a Team Sport – Play It to Win!*, Anclote Press, 2003

Five

The
Dynamically Stable Enterprise:
Engineered for Change

By Vasile Buciuman-Coman & Adrian George Sahlean
(Adapted from *The Dynamically Stable Enterprise*, Meghan-Kiffer Press)

INTRODUCTION: *Vasile Buciuman-Coman and Adrian George Sahlean explore the ramifications of offshore manufacturing and IT outsourcing; a topic of significant concern and interest to BPM initiatives as many organizations struggle with the question of "Should I outsource business processes, and if so, which ones?"*

"You can engineer the enterprise just like you can engineer anything else"
—John Zachman

Offshore manufacturing and IT Outsourcing – is this the future of the enterprise? In a *Business Week* article, "The three scariest words in U.S. industry: The China Price,"[1] an international procurement vice-president expressed what many businesses are increasingly worried about: "The reason practically all home furnishings are now made in China factories is that they simply are better suppliers. American manufacturers aren't even in the same game." This quote is about furniture, but, can this also be the future of more advanced industries like automotive, or computer networking?

A hundred years ago, America's challenge was to manufacture products in a way that was affordable for everyone. Henry Ford invented the assembly line and, ever since, manufacturing has never been the same. Even in the most sophisticated microprocessor plants (fabs) today, where advanced electronic circuits are manufactured, Henry Ford would feel at home. Ford's assembly line, together with Alfred Sloan's superior management techniques, brought U.S. manufacturing, based on standardization and mass production, into modernity. For an entire century, America reached into the assembly line bags of tricks and created faster, cheaper, better products than everybody else.

With the beginning of the new century a new challenge lies ahead for the American manufacturing. *The world caught up with our learning, and manufacturing is no longer a competitive advantage for the American economy.* Low-cost offshore manufacturing and outsourced services challenge the new generation of engineers to find new ways to compete. Services may replace some of the lost ground, but more and more the foundations of the American economy, created by the ingenuity of generations of engineers, have eroded. A new thinking is needed to build the next competitive advantage into America's manufacturing and it may be based on another American great invention, Information Technology. Searching for the Next Big Thing, lean manufacturing, computers, advanced operating systems and the Internet are all part of the new approach, but they alone are not enough to achieve that competitive advantage. *Many of these new technologies are used today simply to 'do' the same things faster, not better.* How these things can be put together is similar to assembling a box of electronic components to make a radio, instead of using them to build higher value microprocessors. The resulting value is different. The enterprise needs to be reinvented again, like Henry Ford reinvented manufacturing a hundred years ago by taking advantage of all existing ideas at that time. The new enterprise should bring a dramatic new vision about how to manufacture better, cheaper, faster products by using the processing of information as the new competitive advantage.

"No industry builds wealth the way manufacturing does, with its layers of added value," notes one of the readers of Business Week.[2] This speaks to the core issue, since while almost everyone agrees that the economic trend is toward services, manufacturing remains a key factor. Some economists even predict that the nation is at the forefront of another revolution that will transition into a completely service-oriented economy with all the manufacturing done overseas! In our view, this is very unlikely.

An enterprise that develops, manufactures and sells new products, together with added services, revolves around two major transformations: Knowledge into Product, and Product into Customer Value. If we analyze a product lifecycle, the role of services in manufacturing comes between these two transformations. Controlling how services are provided always entails controlling the development of new products. *However, the development of new products always lashes back into enterprise operations, and that includes manufacturing, product selling and its customization.*

Tight integration of manufacturing into the enterprise of the future is not the only trend. What Henry Ford said many years ago: "there is one rule for industrialists and that is: make the best quality of goods possible at the lowest cost possible, paying the highest wages possible," is still valid today. In the 21st century. However, we should add: "make the best quality products faster while providing best services tailored to each customer." *The future of the enterprise is consumer-tailored product-manufacturing and integrated services—done here, in the U.S.!*

To build an enterprise on what each customer needs—at a competitive cost, at the highest quality possible, and in an acceptable timeframe—necessitates a bird's eye perspective of both the enterprise and the value chain it serves.

The Enterprise as an Abstract Concept: Processes, Business Entities and the Value Chain

Peter Drucker, the management guru, described the company as "a reality for shareholders, for creditors, for employees and for tax collectors. But economically, it is fiction. What matters in the marketplace is the economic reality, the costs of the entire process, regardless of who owns what." This is as true now as it was then, and it will stay true for the foreseeable future. Cost advantage has indeed been one of the most important ways to deliver value to the customer. However, listening to the customer's demands—and following them closely and faster— together with external factors like environmental concerns, are currently shaping the enterprise in ways divinatory for the 21st century.

In his book, *The Fifth Discipline,* Peter Senge dwells on the discipline of building mental models. An adequate model requires the use of knowledge in a way that makes it explicit to others, but also unique in its ability to synthesize existing concepts. A unifying enterprise model should integrate all the elements of the enterprise, from the simple to the highly sophisticated, which apply to all businesses.

The enterprise, seen as an *abstract* entity, encompasses the main components encountered in the *real* enterprise: business entities (knowledge, product, and customer), business processes (operations and process management), value chain (product and information flows), decision-chain (drives change), and the technology that enables processes to be efficient and flexible. The entire enterprise is driven externally by: a) the business plan model, or how the customer value is generated; b) the available resources; c) the external business factors of change like market and legislation; and d) the technology lifecycle. The above drivers and components are found in all real enterprises, from the simple boutique to the largest corporation.

As shown in Figure 1, the highest-level enterprise model presents all the major enterprise components and drivers, and how the relationships among them can create different viewpoints at the next level of detail.

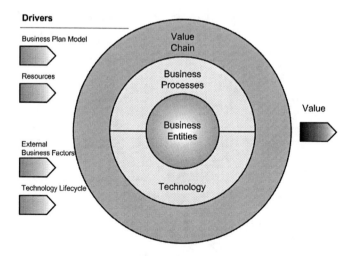

Figure 1: The enterprise model—business entities, processes, value chain and technology with the main drivers

At this level, the generic enterprise is based on three main views:

- *Value Chain (vs. Processes).* The value-chain view captures the three main flows: product, product information and decision chain. The product flow captures how a *product* is assembled during its lifecycle, while the product information flow captures how *information* is assembled to support the product transformation process. The decision chain drives the change of enterprise processes.

- *Business Entities (vs. Processes)*. There are three main business entities: Knowledge, Product, and Customer lifecycles. These entities support the two main enterprise transformations of Knowledge into Product, and Product into Customer Value.

- *Technology (vs. Processes)*. There are two types of processes: Operations and Business Process Management. How the technology is used to enable them determines the enterprise efficiency and agility. *Operations* handle mainly the product and product information flows and answers the questions: *Who, Where,* and *When.* The Business Process Management handles mainly the decision chain and answers the questions *Why, How,* and *What.*

The view of the value chain includes two main elements (product and product information) linked together by business events.

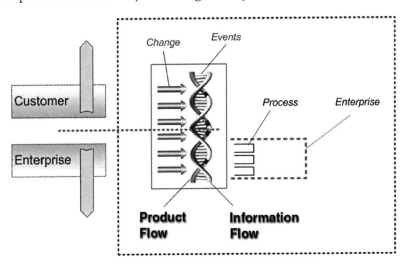

Figure 2. The Value-Chain (vs. Processes) view of the enterprise

As Figure 2 shows, at every step in the value chain, products are being processed based on the available information. The process is the essence of the product and information flows, while the enterprise represents the independent unit for creating value. Both external and internal factors of change are constantly at work, reshaping both value chain processes and the enterprise.

In the value chain, *Operations,* addressing the questions *Who, When,* and *Where,* are linked to the processes that drive execution. *Business Process Management (BPM),* addressing the questions *Why, How,* and *What,* is linked to the processes that drive decision-making. BPM uses information generated by business events to generate a strategy that will introduce operational change in the enterprise.

From the viewpoint of business *entities,* Knowledge drives the entire enterprise. Product and Customer are the other two major entities.

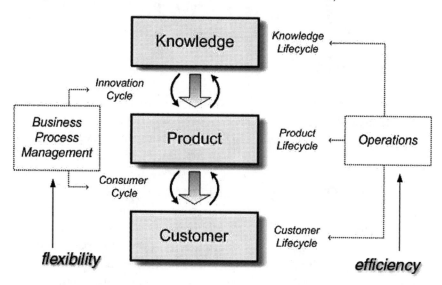

Figure 3: The Business Entities (vs. Processes) View of the enterprise

The above figure presents the two enterprise transformations (Knowledge into Product or 'the innovation cycle' and Product into Customer Value or 'the consumer cycle') that are both part of *BPM.* The lifecycles of Knowledge, Product, and Customer capture the *Operations.* Because the innovation cycle defines how the enterprise adapts to new products, while the consumer cycle how its products adapt to customer needs, they combine to determine the enterprise's *flexibility* in adapting to the economic environment. *Efficiency* is determined by *Operations*.

The third viewpoint of Technology is presented in Figure 4. Its role is to help increase productivity for both BPM and Operations.

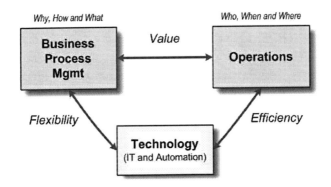

Figure 4. The Technology View (vs. Processes) of the enterprise

What has the part played by technology been so far? During the last century, breakthroughs in technologies (engineering, especially automation) took the concept of the assembly line from simple repetitive tasks to the latest lights-out microprocessor fab. But as we cross the threshold to fierce 21st century competition, we are seeing another revolution emerging, with IT enabling productivity for the next leap forward. In the new playground, dimensions like 'from sensor to boardroom' and 'from idea to product end-of-life cycle' intuitively describe the complexity of the enterprise environment. As a result, a top-down approach to bridging business processes, technology and customer value is needed. The model should achieve high efficiency and flexibility for the value chain *at the same time*, and this is what the Dynamically-Stable Enterprise (DSE) framework aims to do.

The DSE tenet is that the two most fundamental drivers for the value chain are a) *efficiency*, driving productivity, the main indicator of economic progress; and b) *flexibility or adaptability*, driving the ability to adapt to customer requirements, introduce new products and services, and build new technology platforms around the product lifecycle.

As we enter the Information Age, any enterprise solution should address the demands of both drivers. Currently, businesses aim for efficiency only by refining their *Operations* and once that is achieved, further change is avoided because it would require yet another refinement to optimize overall efficiency. Thus, the flexibility challenge is to engineer the entire enterprise for *change*.

If we use a simple analogy and compare enterprise Operations with a plane (see Figure 5), we can distinguish a *highly-efficient* type—similar to a transportation plane—and a *highly-adaptive* type—similar to a fighter plane. Dell is an example of enterprise where efficiency plays a crucial role. From taking the order to delivering a computer, every step is carefully analyzed to maximize efficiency of the overall operations. At the other end of the spectrum, an example of flexible operations is the hospital emergency room. Every patient comes with a unique problem, and finding a solution and applying it must be done within minutes. Thus, operations flexibility in an emergency room needs to be at its highest.

As with the plane analogy, the more stable an enterprise, the more efficient its operations—but the more difficult to change. During 70s, a new concept was developed that allowed building a plane that was efficient and adaptive at the same time. This concept, called the *dynamically-stable configuration*, was applied to the Blackhawk, one of the most advanced planes in the world. The plane was designed to have its operations *unstable*, and it used technology (a computer checking its configuration continuously) to maintain its course. When the plane needed to change direction, it is the *instability* that made it possible to happen extremely fast. Every change of direction became fast and efficient.

A similar approach can be applied to the enterprise operations and management. You can first make enterprise operations flexible by preparing them for change, and use technology to achieve high efficiency. Next, process management can be made efficient by applying a very rigorous structure, and technology can be used to respond quickly to business changes. The entire enterprise (both operations and process management) can thus be made both flexible and efficient. Our Dynamically-Stable Enterprise concept captures this two-pronged approach.

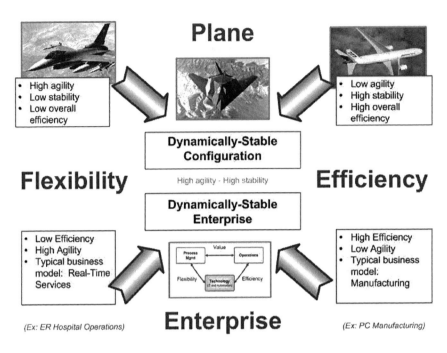

Figure 5. The Dynamically Stable Enterprise Analogy

How to Digitize the Entire Enterprise

During the last century productivity increased five times, with an average growth of 2-3% every year. This was made possible only through the automation of enterprise operations. The constant increase in productivity started with the introduction of the assembly line by Henry Ford. Later on, superior management techniques introduced at GM by Alfred Sloan, integrated the assembly line into the overall enterprise process structure.

In the assembly line, information about the product (e.g., quality control) is inherently generated at every step. This information flow also lies at the basis of decision-making. Product flow is seen as a *complete* lifecycle, from raw material to recycling or product disposal.

Separating the different roles of information in driving product flows vs. the decision chain is almost impossible. Yet, current approaches to information processing are focused mainly on solving either one or the other. For instance, almost all existing enterprise applications manage information locked up in data center vaults that use a static model. However, there's an increased recognition that the next generation of applications needs to *free* the information. Adam Bosworth, widely recognized as a pioneer in the development of XML, recommended recently[3] that applications be moved from the well-understood and increasingly static area of scaling relational databases, to the use of an enterprise *Information Bus* that will store, route, query, filter, manage and interact with information.

Another new concept, grid computing, recognizes the need for processing to be distributed across many applications. Although grid computing points to a future model wherein connectivity plays a key role, process complexity is ignored.

Within the on-demand model (an outsourced model), Marc Benioff, CEO of Salesforce.com, qualifies enterprise IT as drowning in complexity.[4] However, by separating IT from the business, on-demand does not address the intimate relationship between information, product flow, and the role of information as a factor of change.

Any new concept that tries to automate information processing must address these three main areas:

1. the dual role played by information within the decision chain;
2. the universal access to that information and the users' roles;
3. the flow of product information and the decisions driven by the overall process structure;

Each one of these areas presents specific challenges:

1) Despite certain progress, *automation of the decision-making process is still a desideratum*. As seen in the Figure 3, the business entities and their transformations, there are two key steps in the decision-making chain, i.e. when a new product is introduced into manufacturing, and when it is sold to a customer. In these steps, information processing is currently not integrated in a lock-step fashion because the intersection of the two key steps has been difficult to automate. Engineering Change Management typically covers the first step, and the difficulty to automate it lies in the complex relationship between Operations and Business Process Management. For the second transformation, the Internet revolutionized the selling process, by bridging the information flow between the

enterprise and the customer. However, outside the simple communication between customer and business during selling, little has been done in automating how a new customer is acquired, or how a product is serviced or upgraded, despite the fact that this is what truly produces value.

2) The challenge is to provide *universal access to information processing*—decision-making and product flow information—because the goal of enterprise automation is to increase productivity for all business participants. Two important obstacles are involved: first, to solve the complexity of interface design, because, as the automation level increases, the level of complexity makes increased productivity more difficult for the user; and, second, to provide the actual point of access to all processes that empower the individual role in the enterprise.

On the bright side, there are only four major user roles: business operator, business analyst, manager and technologist. Each role has a very specific set of interfaces to enterprise processes. Automating access to operations through interfaces based on user *role* is very similar to how computer operating systems hide the complexity of computer operations from the user. Based on this analogy, we call the DSE infrastructure—that targets full digitizing of the enterprise, hiding the complexity of processes from a participant—the *Operating System of the Enterprise.*

However, providing points of access to all business participants is possible only if all equipment is made *information-aware*, that is, capable of providing personalized and very friendly interfaces to all enterprise processes. For instance, an operator should not be required to learn Excel in order to access product quality reports.

3) From the viewpoint of processes, the challenge is to automate the three main flows—product, information and the decision chain. Since the information flow follows closely the product flow, and the decision chain needs to be integrated at every step, the concept of assembly line—already successful in automating the product flow—can be extended to include the other two flows. Thus the *Operating System of the Enterprise* can also be named the *integrated assembly line.*

Because complexity will permeate the future enterprise, automation needs to address complexity itself. For a very long time, traditional engineering has used a top-down, complexity-based, layered approach to solve the problem of complexity. The DSE uses the same approach.

Eventually, as enterprises become more complex, IT will drive the next wave of automation focused on Business Process Management, and on enabling all workplaces to access the information related to decision-making and product flow.

Why it is so difficult to digitize the entire Enterprise?

In a Business Week article,[5] George Jones III, president of Seaman Paper Co., maker of crepe and decorative paper, described the current attempt to allay competitiveness problems through automation as follows: "We thought we could offset Chinese labor cost by automating, but we just couldn't.... The Chinese imports are selling below Seaman's cost of materials." How can we compete with this?

In the same article, John D. Basset III, CEO of Vaughan-Basset, a furniture manufacturer, mentions that despite the fivefold increased productivity of its 600-worker Galaxy plant (by investing in computer-controlled wood drying, cutting, and carving gear) both sales and workforce have shrunk. The high tech industry is in no better shape. Michael E. Marks, CEO of Flextronics Corp., a contract manufacturer, puts it bluntly: "All electronics hardware manufacturing is going to China." Even the microprocessor industry, with practically unlimited budgets, does not fare any better. The lights-out factory, where operation automation has reached the highest level, every time a new generation is introduced the entire infrastructure must be replaced at a very high cost.

In other industries, like car manufacturing, despite the fact that the labor cost to assemble a car is now reduced to a couple of hundreds dollars, car prices have, paradoxically, gone up. The same has happened in airplane manufacturing. Despite greatly increased productivity, airplane manufacturing costs have gone up, only partially determined by the increased complexity of the products. This, however, only underscores that the current approach to automating complexity driven by increasing the efficiency of information processing has run out its course.

Despite overall advances in automation, there are industries where productivity increase is almost zero. This is the case of healthcare, where information drives the entire process, but where traditional IT platforms like ERP (Enterprise Resource Planning) failed to make a difference.

All of the above points to a single conclusion. Attempting to automate the enterprise by increasing productivity of its operations alone is not good enough anymore. The traditional assembly line bag of tricks is now empty. Moreover, there are only very few choices: we either ascribe to a model where low cost labor will dominate the market (thereby also giving up leadership in the world economy), or we move to the next generation of enterprise automation that can take us beyond just increasing productivity in operations. Unfortunately, the first alternative is not an option as slave-level wage earners in other countries outnumber us. The innovation needed to move to the next generation of enterprise automation will require not only *leadership* but also a new *vision*.

But why it is so difficult to fully digitize the entire enterprise? It is obvious that IT is the key, and information processing is the main focus. When we look at IT's role in automating the enterprise, we see that so far the focus has been rather one-sided. All advanced automation solutions, like the assembly line, Manufacturing Resource Planning (MRP), or Enterprise Resource Planning (ERP) platforms, are applied to increase *Operations* efficiency only, and they do very little to address enterprise flexibility. To move forward and seek a new source of competitive advantage, IT implementations must also support the *BPM* processes.

The bottom line is that as products and value chains increase their complexity, the demands for higher quality products introduced at a faster pace, together with services, requires an approach to automation that is long term. A top-down approach, layering processes and interfaces based on taming complexity, should result in an infrastructure capable of addressing the longer-term goal of handling ever-increasing complexity. Digitizing the enterprise is difficult mainly because the decision chain that drives flexibility is very hard to automate, and building the information-aware equipment that empowers the user is a long term, costly investment. We need a more practical approach.

DSE addresses this by building an infrastructure where, at every step, business participants can access information allowing them to be efficient, and also access the tools empowering them to *act* on that information, and thus become part of the decision chain.

Building the DSE infrastructure may take years—the code base underlying the six BPM and the four Operations (Interface) layers can involve billions of code lines (the Web browser is a good example)—but the good news is that the emerging BPM technologies, the direction of development and the already implemented components will have little need for change.

Here's an illustration of the DSE vision applied to house building (while the house is the biggest expense in someone's lifetime, house construction is one of the least automated processes). The development of new construction equipment still targets automation of operations, yet integrating it with the automation of process management is completely ignored. Even modular houses continue to be built using traditional technologies without integrating process management information.

The DSE approach for this field envisions the integration of tools and other equipment into a single platform driven by architectural specs, through common interfaces built on a single infrastructure (thus making them information-aware equipment.) Materials would be pre-built for automated assembly and would have bar-coded information (or RFID tags) for their integration with process management. All construction equipment would become information-aware, and provide the user with complete information on the project, schedule, environment, materials used, assembling instruction, blueprints and collaboration tools that provide access to the architect, finances, leasing and the entire network of the construction team (plumbing, electrical, carpentry, etc). This scenario would lower the cost of house construction by a full order of magnitude.

To sum up, automating process management in the enterprise would ultimately create the foundation for competing effectively in the 21st century. It will also be the stepping-stone toward the next generation of enterprise, the customer-driven enterprise.

Informatization of the Enterprise: The Third Wave

A long, long time ago, when customers wanted a product of highest quality made quickly, they had to choose a top craftsman. Then came the *industrial revolution* and the choice was not only greater but the price was also significantly lower. However, it was only after the flexible assembly line was invented (exemplified by the now-famous Toyota production system) that both choice increased and price dropped dramatically for all kinds of products, from simple to complex ones.

The entire process of automation has now reached the stage where lights-out factories use the latest generation of robots, with almost no manpower, to work at the assembly line. However, the entire knowledge about how the product is manufactured (the information point-of-view) is stored at the time when the assembly line is configured. This creates a major flexibility problem for the entire enterprise, since future changes in both processes and technology will be extremely hard to implement. For this reason, automating Operations to raise productivity started to fade out as the major source of competitive edge. In a way, we reached a stage similar to the transition from steam engine to internal combustion. The former had run its full course, and the new generation of locomotion needed the superior efficiency and flexibility of the latter. Obviously, a new approach is needed.

For the enterprise, the new generation of superior locomotion started when the *Third Wave*[6] was born, and technology used in automating information processing. The focus is now shifting from the automation of Operations to the automation and complete lifecycle management of business processes.

The new 'wave' has followed a path similar to industrialization: once computers and networking were in place, available and reliable, best business practices were integrated into products like Manufacturing Resource Planning (MRP) or Enterprise Resource Planning (ERP) platforms. Later, standardization made its way and was targeting both *interfaces*—the Internet was the first major standard bridging the information flow between the enterprise and its customers—and *information processing*—the workflow process is standardized by organizations like WfMC. Existing enterprise applications were in turn required to provide support for the new standards. Their evolution was also removed from the control of software vendors, thus ensuring their openness.

Over time, this process led to the building of standardized infrastructures, like Java 2 Enterprise Edition (J2EE) and Microsoft .NET, which use plug-in components to run and build enterprise applications.

The DSE, with its layered architecture, provides a clear path for the process of *informatization* or *informating* the enterprise, which is nothing but the incremental automation of the *Operations* and *Business Process*

Management layers. The goal of DSE is to digitize the entire enterprise, by providing the blueprint for building an integrated open-standard infrastructure, on top of which custom-built components would enable all processes. As a result, each business participant, by using information-aware equipment, would have full access to the information flow and the decision-making.

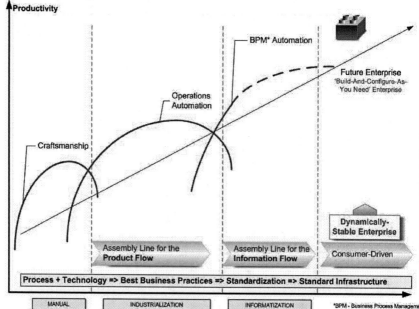

Figure 6. Evolution of the Enterprise: From Craftsmanship to Industrialization to Informatization (the Third Wave)—to Consumer-Driven

By fully digitizing the entire enterprise (*informatization*), the new Dynamically-Stable Enterprise becomes extremely efficient and flexible. Such an enterprise will be prepared to respond directly to consumer requests based on their preferences. Building the DSE will represent the *consumer-driven fourth 'wave,'* and this can go all the way into the 22nd century. At that stage, a product based on individualized consumer requirements will be manufactured with parts and services from different enterprises, as fast and as easy as today's news is generated, assembled, and displayed as a unit, despite the fact that it is gleaned from different Web sites.

Efficiency vs. Flexibility: The 21st Century Dilemma

Maximum efficiency dominated the way productivity was understood during the last century. A company like Dell became a poster child of the efficiency model. Supply-chain frameworks, fine-tuned at each and every step, made sure that every penny was spent wisely. Most innovations were introduced to manufacture cheaper products. Information processing (a flexibility driver) was mostly either ignored—because there were no immediate benefits—or simply downgraded to a lower importance.

Wall Street is pressuring for more efficiency while the market demands new products and better services. How to automate the entire enterprise by balancing these two drivers is the goal of the 21st century. The dilemma between efficiency and agility solved by aircraft engineers in the 'Blackhawk' will inspire enterprise architects to build efficiency and flexibility into a more comprehensive solution for enterprise automation.

Various attempts were made to address both efficiency and flexibility (process management and operations) in the last three decades (see figure 7).

In enterprises where flexibility lies at the core of their business, traditional approaches to improve efficiency have failed. The healthcare industry, for instance, had little success in countering the huge cost increases in recent years through cost cutting.

However, solving the dilemma between efficiency and flexibility does not entail a 'one-size-fits-all' approach. The DSE captures both the contradictory nature of the two drivers and how they apply differently to the various types of businesses.

Based on the six DSE layers that fully support BPM—transactional, interprocess, functional, cross-functional, adaptive, knowledge—there are only four major business plan models. They capture the entire variety of existing businesses, regardless of their industry vertical. These are (in order of complexity):

- *Service Process-Driven.* The operations are built around transactions. It is the simplest of all, where each customer request triggers a process execution. The perfect examples are bank or shipping companies.

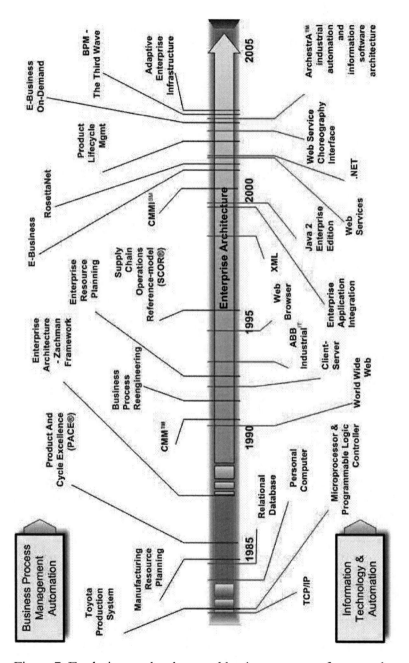

Figure 7. Evolution: technology and business process frameworks

- *Operationally Efficiency-Driven.* The operations are built around product manufacturing where cost is the main driver. The perfect example is a car manufacturer, where cutting cost is the main goal.
- *Innovation-Driven.* The operations are built around developing new products. The perfect example is the pharmaceutical industry, where R&D drives its operations.
- *Service Customer-Driven.* The operations are built around every customer needs. This is the most complex of all. The perfect example is hospital operations, where every patient would be ideally treated as an individual case.

A strong relationship exists between these four fundamental business models. They tend to evolve from the simple one to the next one in complexity, with the tendency to move from high-efficiency to high-flexibility. The DSE addresses the challenge to maintain the high-efficiency of the lower complexity models as they evolve into the highly-flexible. An illustration is provided by successful retailers (like Wal-Mart) who are now adding product manufacturing to their businesses while preserving operations efficiency. Another example comes from car manufacturers, who have reduced the development of a new vehicle from five years to three years; they made innovation a main driver, while maintaining the same cost for their entire operation.

However, the biggest problem with using technology to automate processes on efficiency alone is that, when processes change, you also have to change the solution. When flexibility is considered, the solution can be changed on the technology lifecycle instead of the process lifecycle. The technology lifecycle is many times slower, which makes the investment in technology many times more efficient. For instance, a new generation of microprocessors comes out every four or five years, while processes related to the introduction of new products may change every year. Considering the size of the IT industry alone, this 'simple' change in how flexibility is viewed can entail staggering savings.

Focusing on efficiency alone can be an exercise in frustration: every time a new product is fine-tuned, new marketing initiatives (or a new strategy) will entail the fine-tuning of the entire automation platform. This process is not only costly, but also time consuming.

The dilemma of efficiency vs. flexibility needs a solution that targets higher flexibility while maintaining maximum efficiency.

Types of Change that Drive Flexibility

Enterprise flexibility is measured by the ability to react to change fast so that the same level of efficiency is maintained. Normally, the bigger the change, the higher the risk and the cost. Ideally, increasing flexibility would transform the implementation of a major change from a high-risk, high-cost proposition into a low-risk, low-cost solution. Figure 8 presents the two types of enterprise change based on their driving processes:

- *Process Management Change.* It covers two types, *cyclical* (e.g., new product development) and *non-cyclical* (e.g., technology upgrades or mergers and acquisitions).

- *Operational Change.* It covers three types, *business driver* (e.g., new investment), *reference model* (e.g., new markets or services) and *process optimization* (e.g., technology reconfiguration).

The ideal change is process optimization, since it is low-risk and low-cost. By increasing flexibility, all changes should be targeted to become of the process optimization type. Mark Evans, CIO of Tesoro Petroleum, confronts this directly in a recent article:[7] "When it came to automating these [enterprise] processes, roughly 10% is in implementing the technology, the other 90% is change and process management."

The greatest effort in the enterprise relates to *change management*. Making the enterprise flexible, will not only lower the effort, it will also make it low-risk.

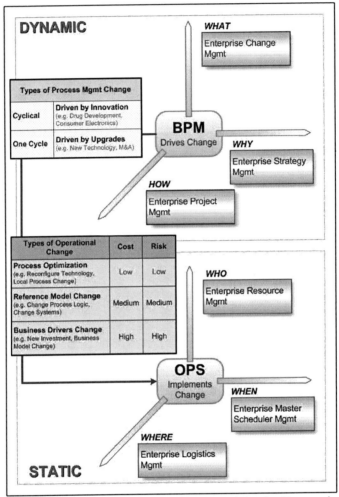

Figure 8. Types of Change (vs. Processes) in the Enterprise

Dilemma Solved: the Dynamically-Stable Enterprise

We have concluded that an ideal approach would not only build efficiency and flexibility into the entire enterprise, but it should also be generic enough to apply to any business, irrespective of its size and business plan model.

In the previous section we compared the enterprise to a plane that is selectively responsive to changes. We viewed the plane as a dynamic system and extended the analogy to the enterprise. The *Dynamically-Stable Enterprise* views the enterprise as a *dynamic system,* with static and dynamic dimensions, which revolves around the three main business entities: knowledge, product and customer.

In a dynamic enterprise, the static dimension is given by the *structure* of processes; it entails the corresponding (static) processes of 'knowledge lifecycle', 'product lifecycle', and 'customer lifecycle.' The *dynamic* dimension is given by the *behavior* of the enterprise processes; it covers mainly the transformations of knowledge into product, and of product into customer value.

The challenge in automating the enterprise is precisely the ability to integrate the static and the dynamic dimensions of all processes into a single infrastructure. Figure 9 presents the DSE as a generic dynamic system, while Figure 10 illustrates the next level of detail.

The dynamic model is inspired by the pioneering ideas developed over 20 years by Stafford Beer. *The Heart of the Enterprise,*[8] a work capturing his ideas during the seventies, describes the enterprise as a *Viable System Model* whose main driver is change. The *Viable System Model* failed to define, however, a way in which technology can be integrated to support change, and it ignored the *static* dimension given by the structure of the enterprise processes. Examples of (dynamic) processes driving the two transformations are those measuring the *enterprise performance* and those capturing *customer value*. For instance, enterprise performance measures operations (by KPIs) and, at the BPM level, through the model that drives change.

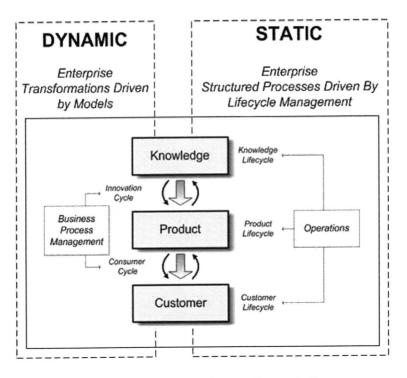

Figure 9. The Enterprise as a Dynamic System

The DSE analysis of the *static* dimension was inspired by process frameworks like *PACE®*[9] and *SCOR®*.[10] PACE is used to describe the product development process, while SCOR is used for supply chain operations. PACE, a proprietary framework developed by PRTM, describes in detail new product development and product portfolio management. SCOR, maintained by Supply Chain Council, with thousands of members worldwide and growing membership, describes in detail the key supply-chain processes and performance parameters. However, both frameworks (implemented and recognized for years as leaders in the field) ignore the transformations that confer the enterprise its *dynamic* dimension and the role played by technology in enabling both types of processes.

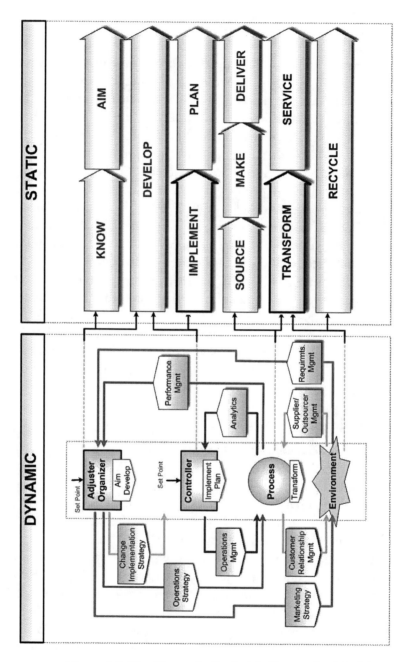

Figure 10. The Dynamically-Stable Enterprise Model

At the highest level, the *static* dimension of the DSE takes the PACE and SCOR frameworks to the next level. It integrates them into a single framework that captures the three lifecycles: Knowledge, Product, and Customer. The high-level structure of enterprise processes always starts with knowledge and skills (KNOW) translated into strategy (AIM). Strategy drives product development (DEVELOP). Once developed, a product (or service) is launched (IMPLEMENT) through change management into operation. At the same time, the product is also scheduled (PLAN) accordingly. Suppliers are providing (SOURCE) materials and parts/subassemblies for product manufacturing (MAKE). Once completed, the product is sold (DELIVER) to existing and new (TRANSFORM) customers. During its usage, the product is maintained, repaired, and overhauled (SERVICE). At the end of its lifecycle, the product can be reintroduced in the business cycle (RECYCLE).

The DSE, sitting on top of the generic enterprise model (Figure 1), adds to the above the business drivers that force changes. It applies to any enterprise, regardless of size and type of business plan model.

In a nutshell, the DSE approach will allow businesses to build a *dynamically-stable infrastructure* that acts like an Operating System for the enterprise. The result is an *integrated assembly line* that allows all enterprise business processes to be efficient and adaptable to changes.

DSE–Leading the Way to the Future

While the economic trend is toward services, manufacturing remains a key factor. Low-cost offshore manufacturing and outsourced services challenge businesses to find new ways to compete. Despite economists who predict a completely service-oriented economy with all the manufacturing done overseas and outsourced IT, we think this scenario very unlikely for the following reasons.

Tight integration of manufacturing with the development of new products and extended customized services at a faster pace revolves around BPM. Offshore manufacturing not only slows the pace but also hinders providing customized services. Outsourcing IT is not a solution either, since BPM is driven by IT. Only a highly-efficient and highly-flexible enterprise can tightly integrate IT into BPM, product development, manufacturing and customized service.

DSE proposes this new and comprehensive roadmap to the future. We stress that the DSE does not change the main business model, since efficiency for profit remains the fundamental tenet of any business. Again America is in position to provide leadership in opening new roads to the future of the enterprise. By succeeding in their quest for industrialization, India and China will create new foundations on which the dynamically-stable enterprise (DSE) will become the standard for innovation, where DSE will play a role similar to the 'assembly line' in the last century.

Architecture is one of the oldest engineering disciplines, with history going back thousands of years. However, traditional architecture dealt with *static* structures that, once built, allowed for very few changes. When architecture and BPM is applied to the enterprise it needs to address also its *dynamics*. Since knowledge, products, customers, and business environment are continuously changing, the architecture needs to introduce change with minimum disruptions to value creation. DSE or any other methodology at the enterprise level will have to support and describe in detail the enterprise structure, its dynamics, how to increase value, and how to respond to drivers like legislation, market pressure, and so on.

Our prediction is that in ten years from now enterprise architecture based on a DSE-like framework will be the only way to manage the enterprise dynamics and its processes (BPM and Operations).

References.

[1] "The three scariest words in U.S. industry: The China Price," Business Week, December 4,2004

[2] "Readers Report," Business Week, December 27, 2004

[3] Adam Bosworth, "Data Routing Rather than Databases: The Meaning of the Next Wave of the Web Revolution to Data Management," Proceedings of the 28th VLDB Conference, Hong Kong, China, 2002

[4] Eric Knorr, "Will these troublemakers put IT out of business?," Inforworld, November 29, 2004

[5] "The three scariest words in U.S. industry: The China Price," BusinessWeek,

December 6, 2004

[6] Howard Smith and Peter Fingar, Business Process Management: The Third Wave, Meghan-Kiffer Press, 2003.

[7] David Kodama, "The New Breed of CIO," Managing Automation, March, 2004

[8] Stafford Beer – The Heart of Enterprise – John Wiley and Sons Ltd, 1994

[9] Michael E. McGrath - Setting the PACE in Product Development, Butterworth-Heinemann, 1996

[10] Supply-Chain Operations Reference-model Version 5.0 – Supply Chain Council Inc., 2001

Six

BPM and "Next" Practice

By Mark McGregor

INTRODUCTION: *In this chapter, Mark McGregor of The Business Process Management Group, takes us forward in our thinking about BPM as he looks at where he sees BPM heading, and how the principles of Business Process Management are destined to become the Key to Real Competitive Advantage.*

In the seemingly never ending quest for improved efficiency, companies are increasingly looking toward "Benchmarking" themselves against their peers, and attempting to apply "Industry Best Practice" to their organizations. Such efforts are being undertaken mainly to enable companies to judge themselves by the standards of their competitors in an attempt to manage costs and deliver matching service. But, "Benchmarking" and "Best practice" will not be enough for many companies; it is only by applying "Next Practice" that they can hope to survive in increasingly global markets. Simply by matching its competition is not a strategy for survival. Western car companies are still struggling financially and yet in most cases have matched the quality levels of their far eastern competitors. In order to survive companies must be more innovative and strive to create "disruptive" change in their markets. Ideally, to create "mini monopolies" which enable periods of rapid growth before the competition catches up, then when they do to move on and create another and so on and so forth.

The Traditional View

Most companies have completed the tasks of mapping their business processes to a greater or lesser extent, at least in some domains of their business. Many such exercises have been undertaken due to regulatory or compliance requirements such as Sarbanes Oxley and Basel II.

Others have recognized that "you can't change what you can't see" and that process mapping serves as a visual roadmap for business and process improvement.

Whatever the initial motivation for greater existing process understanding, the second step for many has been to utilize such maps to attain a greater understanding of the numbers involved. Inevitably, as companies do this they realize that the performance indicators they have traditionally used are not the ones that are most effective in managing the business. Most indicators within organizations have been geared around functions and activities i.e. they are geared to measuring what people do and not toward the customer or process outcomes/effectiveness. Once the appropriate measures and indicators have been identified and recorded it is possible to start running activity based costing or simulations to test the "What if Scenarios" prior to change, or indeed to simply monitor business activity, for example, through the use of digital dashboards.

It is logical that having captured the numbers for the business that such numbers might be used to try and test how an organization compares with others in the same industry or sector – to "Benchmark" the current situation. The desire to "benchmark" can be seen through the levels of interest in frameworks such as SCOR (Supply Chain Council Reference Model) and eTOM (The Telemanagement Forum Telecom Model). These frameworks make it easy for companies to compare themselves with others either in their industry or carrying out similar processes. In addition to "Benchmarking" the comparison also enables companies to see what level of attainment might be achievable by applying "Best Practice" their own organization.

Having mapped, measured, benchmarked and used best practice to understand where the gaps lie it makes sense (based on traditional thinking) to then fire up one or more process improvement projects to address the issues raised. It is here that the problems start to arise.

Traditional process efforts being undertaken in most organizations are still being carried out on a piecemeal basis. The various techniques such as Six Sigma, Lean Service, TQM, and ISO 9000 are being applied on a project basis. They are being used as the "headache" tablets for business, a point of "pain" is identified and then the single technique is used to resolve it. However, most organizations are applying the same "tablet" repetitively regardless of the symptoms and are not making use of the variety of techniques required, and in a holistic manner so as to enable them to bring together such efforts.

The push toward measurement, and judgment based on such measures is to be applauded. It has long been argued that "you can't change what you can't see and you can't manage what you can't measure." What can be questioned is what use should be made of such visualizations and how organizations can or should be managed based on the measures in place.

Perhaps the greatest use of benchmarking is as a communication tool. It can provide something concrete, something that can be taken back to the executive board to demonstrate why things need to change.

Current thinking around "Benchmarking" and "Best Practice" is flawed and in the context of Business Process Management, completely misses the opportunities that BPM affords.

Business Process Management, as has been argued before, is all about enabling companies to be run in new ways and to enable rapid change – either to respond to market changes or to allow fast entry into new areas of business. To date, much emphasis has been placed on the utilization of BPM to fuel the quest for "Cheaper, faster, better" an approach which can only have limited scope in the quest for corporate survival. Why a "limited scope"? Well put very simply, if everyone chases "cheaper, faster, better" and benchmarks themselves against each other there comes appoint of diminishing return. More importantly, in any given market the chances are that a new entrant will come in and do things completely different and play by a different set of rules. Changing the rules in a market has many effects, it can ensure that instead of innovating competition has to play catch up – thus ensuring that valuable resources are used in non-competitive ways. It can completely change customer expectation and massively alter buying habits – witness the amount of goods now bought and sold via online auction companies. In this scenario, simply playing "cheaper, faster, better" will not help companies survive.

The Alternative

It would be unreasonable to suggest that the "cheaper, faster, better" approach will not deliver business benefits. There are numerous examples of companies that have significantly reduced their cost base, improved product quality and improved their speed to market.

Much of this improvement will have been gained though simply undertaking a business process mapping exercise. Experience shows that the single the act of trying to capture how people actually do the work in an organization will lead to immediate and easy to implement changes. The benefit of these changes will in most cases outweigh the cost of carrying out such exercises. The risk is that enthusiasts will suggest that such an exercise should be carried out in detail for all processes in an organization. In reality doing "just enough" tends to be the approach that gets greatest traction within an organization and the greatest level of support from senior management.

The benefits gained from using business process mapping and spotting the "gotchas" can be viewed as a Stage 1 improvement. The use of this Stage 1 technique in identifying where a company is inevitably leads to very quick (and cost effective) improvements, through the picking off of the "low hanging fruit."

"Benchmarking" will require the capture of numerical information against those processes and activities mapped in the stage 1 improvement. This will highlight the areas that might benefit most from some additional process improvement. Depending on the perspective, measuring against others in a similar field may serve to drive a "Gap Analysis" and act as an initial roadmap for improvement. The detail of any such roadmap will tend to be fleshed out by identifying what needs to be done in order to match the levels attained by those considered as running "Best Practice" in the field. By undertaking "Benchmarking" and applying "Best Practice" organizations will ensure that they are not letting competitors get ahead of them in the market. However, this is still all about doing the same things just "Better, Faster, Cheaper" and should be considered as working at Stage 2 levels of improvement.

There is only so far that companies can go using the techniques of stage 1 and 2 improvements. Technological changes certainly mean that there is considerable cost that can be driven out. The use of workflow and process automation has proven this. It should be a given that in the current climate companies either have or are planning to automate as many of their processes as is possible.

Motorola is often spoken about as an example of success in the area of process improvement. It was one of the early adopters of the Six Sigma approach. Over the years, the company will have saved many millions of dollars through improvement projects using this technique. However, a quick look at the financial press suggests that, as a company, Motorola is not doing that well now. This is probably due in part to the fact that whilst it was carrying out many incremental improvements, it did not link these back to the strategic needs of the company. Or perhaps was so focused on the better, faster cheaper that it did not see the big changes coming.

At this early market phase of BPM it would seem that doing the same things in an automated way is all most people are doing. It is rather like the early stages of the industrial revolution; technology is still being developed and used to do to same things. The technology has yet to be applied in enough creative ways to enable new practices in terms of doing business. It is the idea of doing things differently that will generate Stage 3 improvements. Stage 3 improvements can be thought of as "Next Practice" and it will be seen that although they can be enabled by technology, they are in fact leveraged by thinking outside the norm.

Next Practice

Next Practice is about taking the best practices and applying them in new an innovative ways. Ways that competitors have either not done or not thought of doing yet! The beauty of "Next Practice" is that the ideas are all around; nothing has to be invented to begin the journey. The first step in next practice is to simply change the criteria for "Benchmarking" and "Best practice."

Most companies when looking at benchmarking look at the best of their competitors and judge themselves against these companies. These certainly serves as a reasonable starting point and provides some targets to aim for, but are they really stretch targets? Who does the market leader benchmark against?

The same goes for "Best Practice" applying best practice in business process terms will certainly facilitate improvement and in the eyes of the customer may even be the difference between remaining in business or totally disappearing, but again what about the market leader?

"Next practice" demands that in the first instance that organizations look at the very best companies, in whatever domain are and try to apply their standards in your own domain. For example small software development companies tend to look at how the likes of Microsoft or IBM develop and market software, the challenge is that most of the competitors (assuming that they even look outside their sector) will be doing the same, the result is hardly earth shattering. But what if it looked at others who have built their reputations on delivering high quality R&D products outside of the software development arena, (Pharmaceuticals perhaps?) and copied them? What if it looked to brand based companies such as "Coca Cola" for ideas on marketing, what if it looked at someone like "Amazon" for inspiration on building on-line shops for its products and possibly a company like "McKinsey" as its inspiration for providing service. This example is only an illustration but surely a software company that delivered product to the same quality as a pharmaceutical company and services to the standard of McKinsey, while being as smart at brand awareness as Coca Cola and as easy to buy from as Amazon – would cause more than a few ripples in their marketplace.

The world of commerce is filled with great examples of how to do things better and if only companies would look outside of their own industry, they would learn a great deal. Those that do and then bring those practices into their own industry will be seen as no less visionary than those who came up with truly new ways of doing things, but at considerable cost. Early innovators such as Amazon have paid a considerable cost to create what is now considered as the standard for "one click" shopping, while Dell computers spent millions creating a business model for "mass customization" in the PC marketplace, but now customers see these as accepted ways to purchase goods. In France the car company SMART invested heavily in proving a concept known as the smart box, a concept aimed a providing a single price for your car, its servicing, its insurance, warranty and road tax. These early innovators paid the price in terms of investment and in having to educate the market. Now this has been done and others can leverage such experience without the same levels of risk or investment

The need for "Next practice" is time critical, it is not enough to take the wait and see attitude, others have and have paid the price. More insight into the time criticality aspects of Business Process may be found in Peter Fingar's the Real Time Enterprise." In many industries, companies have left it too late to understand the implications of disruptive practice and as a result many companies will fail. This applies not just too individual companies within an industry sector but to whole sectors. Frequently used is the example of western motor manufacturers, however in a technology focused world, the travel sector is one of the best examples. How many people still use a travel agent to make travel arrangements? Most tend to book with hotels and airlines directly over the internet. So the airlines recognized that the internet could change the way they service customers and save them from paying out commissions to travel agents. Why then did those same airlines not recognize that the same internet could also be used to minimize the need for travel at all?

In the financial sector, it is now common for people to use the internet for banking and to deal with call centers many thousands of miles away. So how long will it be before companies from those far off lands start to do business directly in the local home markets?

Whatever the market sector, it is highly likely that in an increasingly global market that there will be companies from other regions looking to enter new markets. They will not be entering new markets based on being the same, but by looking to see how they can be different. They will not be approaching the market with an "always done it this way" mentality but with a clean sheet of paper and no baggage. Such entrants will cause "disruptive" change in many sectors and markets.

Business Process Management makes it easier

Historically the concept of "Next Practice" has not been easy to apply, the ideas are there for all to see, but to actually apply them has not always been so easy. Largely this is because even though the ideas and principles can easily be identified, without a clear understanding of how things are currently done, combined with a detailed understanding of the assets available such ideas were seen as nothing more than mere dreams in the boardroom.

Business Process based approaches to business have now changed all that. Utilizing the maps and measurements that have often been used to do no more than automate existing processes, it is possible to identify how to apply best practice in your business. This change is now easier than it has been due to a combination of the maturity of the technology available to support and integrate efforts and the recognition that it is not a purely technological issue.

True Business Process Management approaches encompass Strategy, People, Process and Systems. This holistic approach ensures that all the key areas of a business are working in sync, heading in the same direction together.

To date most of the work has centered around systems, with some focus on the related IT processes in a business. As things move forward it will increasingly be seen that the results will have to be tied back to strategy in order to retain executive buy in.

Those companies ensuring that enough time is focused on the people side of their business are the ones that will win through in the end. It will be the people of the organization that will make (or break) any new way of working. Much of the success of South West Airlines is not down to strategy, system or process, but instead is due to its people. South West has the lowest staff turnover in the airline industry and yet is not the highest payer, therefore other things must be right. In a market such as the airline industry good staff relations are paramount.

Companies that have truly embraced the BP paradigm i.e. those which have not only mapped a few processes but have also added strategy and vision to their thinking and put in place education and training such that their people are highly attuned to the concepts of change, will find it much easier and quicker to take on "Next Practice."

"Next Practice" is only the beginning

Some readers may feel that this may apply to other businesses but does not apply to theirs. Either because they see that it is too difficult, just another passing fad or because they feel that no-one else in their industry might do it either.

Others will see that "Next Practice" is only just the beginning, for once a company applies the concept of "Next Practice" in its industry, then surely others will try to follow on the basis that it will now have set the "Benchmarking" and "Best Practice" standards by which its competitors will want to judge themselves.

It will be seen that that having applied "Next Practice" by embedding good Business Process management practices and a culture of change within an organization, it will have only just started to raise the bar. For now, it will be able to couple and uncouple such process and practices in new and innovative ways, ways that could cause great disruption in its chosen marketplace.

The companies are able to cause such constant "disruption" in their markets are the ones that will emerge as the true market leaders. They will be forever creating mini-monopolies with only themselves as the provider in the space and then moving on as soon as the competition catches up.

And the key to success here lies in the ability of companies to successfully embed a culture of change within their organization. To create a culture where staff come to view change as a positive thing and embrace the concept wholeheartedly.

Seven

Process-Powered Self Service: The Next Source of Competitive Advantage

By Dr. Pehong Chen

INTRODUCTION: *After a turbulent first decade, the e-business environment has stabilized and companies are investing in IT for strategic growth. Web-based, process-driven self service is recognized as the next source of competitive advantage, but conventional tools and best practices that require a 12 to 18 month development cycle can't meet the demand. Agile process development is a business imperative. Web process management doesn't replace conventional BPM, but complements it by providing a dynamic, people-centric front-end to back-end automation systems. Dr. Chen illustrates the business benefits of process-driven Web self service with anecdotes and customer examples from his experience as founder and CEO of a pioneering e-business enterprise.*

Evolution of the Web Channel

The evolution of enterprise software applications has gone through three generations that are analogous to the evolution of the electrical power grid. First came the ERP applications of the 1980s. These represent the power generator. Next came the CRM applications and early Web applications for commerce and knowledge management. These represent the power grid. These core information systems require a substantial investment and any change is a complex endeavor. But now that the generator and grid are in place we have an opportunity to turn on a thousand light bulbs at relatively little expense with Web-based self service – software applications that enable customers, employees and partners to conduct interactions and transactions that harness the information, tools and processes in backend systems without human intermediation. This is the third generation of enterprise software applications.

The Web was initially recognized as a powerful channel for information access. That quickly expanded to include transactions and collaboration with other parties involved in the sales process and collaboration between employees via a corporate intranet. As Web activities become more complex, a process engine is required to coordinate and manage interactions, transactions and collaboration in a real-time, high-touch model. For example, if you order some books and they don't arrive, it becomes a three-party issue – the customer, the book vendor and the shipping company.

When interactions, transactions and collaborations go beyond one dimension – when they involve multiple people, multiple timeframes, multiple instances - the next step is to wrap process management around them. Process-powered Web self service allows organizations to do more business over the Web in a very scalable, cost effective way. It also benefits customers by saving them time and improving visibility into processes, which increases their loyalty.

Process-Powered Self-Service

To appreciate the benefits of high touch self service on the Web, consider the low touch model that is more prevalent today. When you apply for a loan online, you input your data and wait for the result to come back. The Web is little more than a modem collecting data and displaying results. The application processing occurs in a "black box." You are no longer a participant in the process. You lose visibility into the process. In this scenario there is no difference between a loan application by Web or by phone.

In a high-touch self-service model, you retain visibility into the process and remain a participant – receiving alerts and notifications at points in the process that require input, decisions or collaboration with others involved in the process. All participants have visibility into status, action items and previous activity relating to the process. Rule-driven aspects of the process move forward without requiring an intermediary.

High touch process-powered self service harnesses the power of the Web to meet the needs of all participants in the process and to dramatically reduce the cost of providing high quality service and support. Some would argue that it also improves on the quality of service available in the high touch intermediary model (see Figure 1) by providing concierge-level service at your desktop. It is an outside-in model that shifts the center of gravity to the people involved in the process – providing customers, partners and employees with processes that respond to their needs rather than requiring them to adapt to your processes.

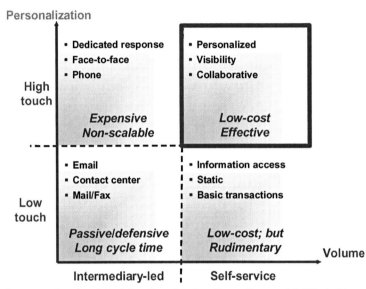

Figure 1: Service Models: Combining Low Cost with High Touch

The Agility Gap

Web-based, process-powered self service is the next source of competitive advantage, but tapping into it requires a new level of agility and a new approach to Web application design and development. A 12 to 18 month cycle for application development will not keep pace with demand or meet business requirements for rapid response to market opportunities.

In the traditional software development model, line of business managers are at the top of the pyramid, business analysts are in the middle, and IT developers are at the bottom. Depending on the company, the middle layer people either belong to the business unit or the IT organization, but it's their job to capture business requirements from the line of business managers and translate them into a software requirements document (SRD) for IT developers to implement.

Although this model is used by 90 percent of companies, most would agree that it does not support an agile development environment. I recently visited with the CTO of a major U.S. bank who said, "We develop our software twice. First our business architects capture all the requirements from our end users and write it down in a Word document. Then the software developers do it one more time in a programming language. Six months later, we find out if they got it right. The worst case scenario is that after a 12 to 18 month development cycle the solution doesn't quite match the business need."

In recent years, offshore outsourcing has added capacity at the bottom of the pyramid. China alone produces over 300,000 Java programmers a year. If you include developers in Europe and India there are close to a million new Java programmers each year. These are very qualified programmers available at one tenth of the cost for U.S. based developers. The business value is compelling, but it only exacerbates the problem of accurately interpreting business requirements during the development phase.

Between heightened demand for Web-based self service at the top of the pyramid and increased coding capacity at the bottom of the pyramid there is a bottleneck. The CIO at a major bank in Taiwan made an interesting comment that underscores this agility gap. "I have 500 people in my IT shop and 3 projects worth several million dollars that I can't even start because I only have five of these business architects and they're totally swamped."

It's not just the agility gap between business requirements and IT execution. Hard coding is hard. It doesn't matter if you are programming in zeroes and ones or assembler or J2EE. Hard coding the business logic and data model requires months or years of development time. And it doesn't matter if you are doing it here or offshore. As Frederick Brooks observed in his classic book The Mythical Man-Month, you can't accelerate childbirth by having nine women produce a baby in

one month and you can't accelerate hard coding by throwing more resources at it.

An Agile Alternative to Hard Coding

New applications are bridging the agility gap by enabling organizations to design and deploy Web-based self-service applications in days
and weeks rather than months and years. The key to this rapid development environment is providing a process lab or workbench that enables
business analysts to create a process model and test process flow prior
to turning the process over to IT for development. Ideally, developers
should be able to use the same tool to enrich the process definition with
adapters to external systems (including backend ERP systems) and to
add specifications for turning design elements into functional Web
pages. This eliminates the confusion and rework time that often result
when developers translate business requirements into code.

Web processes developed in this way can be deployed into existing
Web sites and easily modified – providing a cost effective way for organizations to keep pace with business requirements without the cost
and complexity of a major site overhaul.

Not an Alternative to BPM

Web process enablement doesn't replace business process management. They co-exist. One class of application is for back-end,
"heavy-lifting" processes. The other is for agile front-end, people-centric
applications.

Comparing traditional process management and Web process management is like comparing a ton of lead and a ton of feathers. They both
weigh a ton but the management challenges are very different. One is
very dense. Monolithic. A heavy-duty solution that addresses complex
back-end issues. People are peripheral to these processes.

Web process management, by contrast, is like managing a ton of
feathers. A ton is a ton, but instead of one heavy problem to solve, you
have thousands of edge processes that add up to significant business
value if you manage them effectively.

Both are important. If you put all our energy into automating backend capabilities while ignoring how you present information and serve customers at the front end, the backend investment is wasted. You need both: Traditional BPM on the backend and agile processes on the front end to address time-sensitive market opportunities and solve specific problems.

Traditional BPM	Web Process Management
Focus	*Focus*
Heavy-lifting within back-front office	Self-service around the edges; in the seams
Systems-centric	People-centric
People must adapt to the process	Processes adapt to the people
Mechanical efficiency	People efficiency; time management
End game: eliminate people	End game: engage and empower people
Complex, rigid, daunting	Holistic experience with a human touch
Key Characteristics	*Key Characteristics*
Synchronous	Asynchronous
Deterministic	Non-deterministic
Predictable	Unpredictable
Static	Dynamic
Change is the exception	Change is the norm
IT Paradigm: "Ton of Lead"	*IT Paradigm: "Ton of Feathers"*
Monolithic; oversized footprint	Incremental; solution-driven we-blets
Bottom-up; hard-coded data model and business logic	Top-down; high-level and flexible abstractions
Long development/update cycle	Rapid cycle time
LOB-to-IT bottleneck; agility gap	LOB-to-IT bridge

Figure 2: Traditional BPM vs. Web Process Management

Candidates for Process-Powered Self Service

In studying this problem for the past few years, we have identified three key areas that lend themselves particularly well to Web-based process-driven self service.

Assisted Customer Care

The opportunity here is to use process-powered self service to reduce call center costs and increase customer satisfaction. For example, my son had just turned 19 and our company dental policy says that when a dependent is 19 or older you must show proof of student status every six months to retain coverage. We did not send proof of student status and payment for his checkup was turned down. The dentist didn't get paid for 9 months. There were dozens of phone calls. In the most advanced economy in the world a dispute of $100 takes over $500 to resolve. You could have the most advanced claim processing system in the world on your backend and that would be completely wasted if you couldn't get a $100 bill dispute resolved. It's not just the call center expense. An inefficient process creates frustration and ill will that can lead to customer churn. And, as we all know, acquiring a new customer is 10 times more expensive than keeping an old customer.

Web-based, process-driven self service enables you to rapidly respond to this type of problem, replacing frustration and churn with customer satisfaction and repeat business.

Ad Hoc Collaboration

Another opportunity for process-powered self service is in the area of ad hoc or unstructured collaboration. By modeling and implementing Web-based processes that match your offline processes, you can keep projects on track and on schedule, improve operational efficiency and still allow for creative give-and-take among team members. By moving communications and collaborations from e-mail to Web-based self-service you not only improve productivity, but you preserve institutional knowledge.

One of our manufacturing customers introduces 15 products a year in the U.S. These are not new products; they are already sitting in the warehouse, but it was taking 8-12 weeks to get them to market. The issue was lack of coordination – between marketing, sales, legal, and other groups – and visibility into action items and deliverables. Everybody was in charge and nobody was in charge. By implementing Web-based process management, they've reduced cycle time to 2 or 3 weeks and turned all that chaos into crisp execution and on-time delivery.

Compliance

A third area of opportunity for process-driven self service is policies and compliance. This could be as simple as managing compliance to your company's travel policy or as complex as HIPAA or Sarbanes Oxley compliance. With Web-based process-driven self service, you can build compliance into the structure of the Web application.

Like other public companies, we need to be in compliance with Sarbanes-Oxley. I attended several workshops on this subject and it struck me that many of the solutions miss the point. We put all this effort into capturing our policies and best practices. Then we provide an audit to the SEC at the end of each year to demonstrate our compliance. That leaves a gaping hole in the middle which is the execution of compliance. The important piece – and a great opportunity for Web process management - is to help you implement best practices and enforce compliant in the course of conducting your business.

Assisted Customer Care	Unstructured Collaboration	Policy Compliance
Characteristics:	Characteristics:	Characteristics:
▪ Large number of consumers or clients ▪ High volume/ frequency of issues/cases ▪ Segmented	▪ High number of tasks to coordinate ▪ Widespread across large number of small groups	▪ Large number of complex rules/ regulations ▪ Difficult to follow/comply
Examples:	Examples:	Examples:
▪ Bill/claim dispute resolution ▪ Insurance claims ▪ Device activations ▪ Product returns ▪ Loan applications	▪ Outsourcing (BPO) ▪ Product bundling ▪ Go-to-market management ▪ Channel management	▪ Corporate policy admin ▪ Travel & Expenses ▪ Permit, license, certificate filing/renewal

• Employee benefits management • Incentive/rebate management • Enrollment, warranty renewal • Out-patient services • Benefits enrollment	• Design reviews • Cross-functional projects • Product defect resolution • Merger/acquisition integration • HR on-boarding • HR off-boarding	• Registrations • Capital expenditures • Patient case management • Order management • Credit requests/ authorization

Figure 3: Candidates for Process-Powered Self Service

Conclusion

The opportunities are everywhere. Have you tried to buy a phone and give it to someone as a gift? Five years later you are still on the phone bill. Have you tried to add a process to your HR system? Employee onboarding and offboarding is an issue that our system did not address. When we asked the vendor to provide it to us, they said it would cost another $250,000. It is very hard to change backend systems because the logic is hard coded.

The e-business resurgence has brought with it a huge demand for Web-based self service. Conventional IT tools and best practices won't meet this demand. Agile process development is a business imperative -- not just for developers but also for business architects to break through the IT logjam and bridge the agility gap between business requirements and IT execution.

Eight

Business Rules and Business Processes: Win-Win for the Business

By Ronald Ross

INTRODUCTION: *Business Rules have become an accepted part of the programming requirements for many software products, and BPM software products rely heavily on business rules as a core function of their operation. In this Chapter, Ronald Ross, Executive Editor of Business Rules Journal, discusses the relationship of business rules (the know) and business processes (the flow) in BPM while presenting the true breadth and scope of affect that business rules can have on the creation, operation and maintenance of the truly agile and adaptive organization..*

What is a Business Rule?

In a way, everybody knows what business rules are - they are what guide your business in running its day-to-day operations. Without business rules, you would always have to make decisions on the fly, choosing between alternatives on a case-by-case, ad hoc basis. Doing things that way would be very slow. It would likely produce wildly inconsistent results. I doubt it would earn very much trust from your customers.

In today's world, you cannot really operate that way, at least not for very long. So every organized business process has business rules. But what are they? What exactly do you use to "guide your business in running its day-to-day operations?"

Before we look at a definition of *business rule*, I should be very clear about what business rules are *not*.

Business rules are not software.

Let me be a little more precise. Business rules are often implemented in software, but that is a different matter. Application software is only one of several choices in that regard. Alternative implementation approaches include supporting them in manual procedures (not very efficient but sometimes necessary) or implementing them as rules using a rule engine or decision management platform (a better choice)[1]. The point is that business rules arise as an element of the business, as the name business rules suggests, not from any particular hardware/software platform that supports them.

Business rules are not processes.

Roger Burlton has expressed the business rule message this way, "Separate the know from the flow." The implication is that the "know" part and the "flow" part are different.[2] Business rules represent the "know" part, the separate stuff that guides the "flow." Guidance means rules; hence the name business rules.

Separate the know from the flow.

—Roger Burlton

A good, often quoted definition of "business rule" from the business perspective is the following: "A directive that is intended to influence or guide business behavior. Such directives exist in support of business policy, which is formulated in response to risks, threats or opportunities."[3]

Business rules really mean establishing the "know" part of your business processes as a resource in its own right. This new resource permits changing elements of the "know" part directly, which in turn means being able to change them faster. What business does not want to be able to change faster these days?

Actually, some of the "know" part has always been separated from the "flow" part in the sense that workers carry the "know" part around in their heads. Does such tacit knowledge represent business rules? In one sense, tacit knowledge does represent business rules but in the broader sense of managing business rules, it does not. If you need any proof of that, just think of what happens when the workers retire or go to work for the competition!

For practical purposes, business rules are that portion of the "know" part written down, or better that is encoded, and ready for reuse (or revision) as needed. Here then follows an additional way to describe business rules: *Business rules are literally the encoded knowledge of your business practices.* This encoded knowledge is structured based on terms and facts about the business, and expressed in declarative form so that each bit of business logic is largely self-contained and self-explanatory[4].

Business rules in no way replace business processes – just the opposite, they complement and sharpen them. The goal then is to achieve the right balance between the business processes and business rules, which Burlton might say this way: *"What the company knows should be balanced with its flows."*

Business Rules in the Know

Decision Points

So how do we clarify our understanding of business rules in relationship to business processes? One key is the notion of decision points. A decision point is where some critical decision (usually a complex one) must be made. Such a decision typically might have to do with one of the following kinds of tasks: classification, diagnosis, assessment, monitoring, prediction, assignment, allocation, and so on.

The rules governing such decisions are often particular to, and characteristic of, the company's product/service offerings. These offerings invariably involve the company's special area(s) of expertise. Examples of such decisions include whether or not to:

- Approve an application for automobile insurance
- Pay a claim
- Buy a stock
- Declare an emergency
- Give an on-the-spot discount to a customer
- Assign a particular resource to a given request
- Diagnose a patient as having a particular disease
- Accept a reservation
- Indicate possible fraud

Such decision points, all rule-intensive, are of vital importance to the business. Capturing the relevant rule sets should therefore be a key component of a company's approach to modeling its business processes.

Rejection Points

Decision-making rules are by no means the end of the story in understanding the relation of business processes and business rules. For example, a second and equally important connection pertains to the operational tasks within a business process that proceed and enable an optimal decision to be made at any given decision point. These lead-in tasks produce the data on which basis a sound decision can be made.

In a real business, of course, producing all the data one might use to make a decision can be extremely costly and difficult (and inefficient). Let me offer a simple example. An automobile insurance company might have the following business rule: *An application for car insurance may be approved only if the applicant is at least as old as the minimum driving age.*

This rule, of course, might be only one of hundreds determining whether an application should be approved. Other rules might involve creditworthiness (which could involve an extensive credit check), previous driving history (which could require requesting records from the state), and so on. In other words, a lot of work (time and money) would be involved in gathering all the data required to support all the rules.

Consequently, a basic goal in designing business-friendly business processes is what I call work avoidance (no pun intended). For example, if an applicant for automobile insurance is less than the minimum driving age, why perform the credit check and acquire the driving records? If you can determine up front in the business process that the applicant is too young, all that other data-related work can be avoided.

So, simply capturing all the decision-making rules for each decision point in a business process is clearly not enough for effective support of business systems. "Rejection" rules (such as the minimum driving age rule above) must be coordinated with the business process so they can be tested as soon as possible. Waiting to test them at some downstream decision point is simply inefficient. This early-bird testing of rejection rules is a basic principle of the business rule approach. *To avoid unnecessary work, rejection rules should be tested as early in a business process as possible.*

Process Coordination Rules

Rules that provide the basis for decision points and rejection points within a business process typically have to do with the product/service of the business. However, many business rules exist solely to ensure that the business process itself runs smoothly. Such rules can be called process coordination rules. Examples of process coordination rules versus product/service rules for three different organizations are given below. These rules have been expressed in the declarative rule language, RuleSpeak®.[5] Capturing and managing these business rules separately from the business process model provides the basis for business processes that are 'thin' and much more adaptive.

Process Coordination Rules vs. Product/Service Rules Examples

Internal Revenue Service (IRS)
Process Coordination Rule
Rule: A processed tax return must indicate the IRS Center that reviewed it.
Product/Service Rule
Rule: Calculated total income must be computed as tax return wages (line 1) plus tax return taxable-interest (line 2) plus tax return unemployment compensation (line 3).

Ministry of Health
Process Coordination Rules
Rule: A claim must be assigned to an examiner if fraud is suspected.
Rule: An on-site audit must not be conducted for a service provider any less often than every five years.
Product/Service Rules
Rule: A claim involving comprehensive visits or consultations by the same physician for the same patient must not be paid more than once within 180 days.
Rule: A claim that requests payment for a service event that is a provision of health service type 'consultation' may be paid only if the service event results from a referral received from another service provider.

Ship Inspection Agency
Process Coordination Rules
Rule: A ship inspection work order must include at least one attendance date.
Rule: A ship must indicate a client who is financially responsible for inspections.
Rule: An inspection due for a ship must be considered suspended if the ship is laid up.
Product/Service Rules
Rule: A ship area subject to corrosion must be inspected annually.
Rule: A salt water ballast tank must be inspected empty if the ship is more than five years old.
Rule: A barge must have an approved bilge system to pump from and drain all below-deck machinery spaces.

Smart Processes

Everyone is concerned these days about the accelerating rate of change and the urgent need to build business processes that prove more adaptive. A flip side to the issue of change, however, has received very little attention. That flip side has to do with training.

Remember the old story about telephone operators? In a nutshell, the story goes like this. Use of the telephone in the last century grew at such a fast rate that if automatic switching had not been invented, by now everyone in the world would be a telephone operator. (It didn't happen because digital ('smart') switching was invented.) Growth in the rate of change in business today is just as fast. Workers are being thrown into new responsibilities and procedures at an ever-increasing rate. That means workers must be trained by other workers. If this keeps up, sooner or later everyone in the world will have to become a trainer.

Clearly, that cannot happen. The only solution is to make training automatic ("smart" that is), where training is built right into the business process systems that support the workers' day-to-day responsibilities and procedures. Business rules can make that happen. Briefly, here is how that can be done.

Consider the following rule: A rush order must not include more than five items. Suppose a worker violates this particular rule at an appropriate rejection point within the business process. What error message should pop up on the screen?

Certainly not (as all too often happens today) some obscure system code or message in "computerese." Instead, the initial message should simply be the business rule statement itself. In the business rule approach, we like to say that the business rules are the error messages.

Another way to look at this is that the rule statement represents a requirement that is pure business logic. In the business rule approach, this kind of requirement is incorporated directly when building automated systems to support business processes, then gets output directly to inform the worker when a violation in his or her work is detected. Think of that as a communication from a worker who knows the business logic to a worker who must follow that business logic without these workers ever communicating directly or possibly ever even coexisting in time or space.

A friendly system would go a step further. When an error is detected, the system not only materializes the original business logic for the worker but can also offer a canned procedure so he or she can correct the violation immediately. (This assumes, of course, that the worker is both authorized and capable in all these aspects.)

For the business, this capacity means achieving real-time compliance, eliminating costly downstream detection and corrective action. It means that mistakes can be corrected immediately so they are not compounded as other actions are subsequently taken.

For the individual worker, it means being constantly exposed and re-exposed to the business logic on a highly selective, real-time basis. Remember, the business rule could have been changed just recently, maybe even in the last few seconds.

A smart process is therefore one that supports business rules automatically. By doing so, a smart process can act as a personalized knowledge companion for workers, providing never-ending, on-the-job training. Is there any alternative for keeping harried 21st-century line workers up to speed?!

Addressing Business Goals in Business Process Development

A fundamental aim in developing a sound business process is to ensure it meets business goals. A business process will be of little value if it addresses the wrong ones or addresses the right ones in the wrong way. The key question here is why the business process, in its particular form, is right for the company.

Traditional approaches for developing business systems have not done a very good job of answering that key question. The business rule approach offers a fresh approach. Briefly, the central idea is that achieving business goals[6] always involves a particular set of business risks and inherent conflicts and tradeoffs. Business tactics and core business rules are formulated to address these risks, conflicts, and tradeoffs. These elements of the business solution are structured in a *Policy Charter*[7].

A Policy Charter outlines the business tactics proposed to meet the business goals. The business motivation for each element of business tactics is established. This battle plan offers business sponsors and others a direct view of how the needs of the targeted business process are being addressed. It also permits the following.

- Assessment of business-side feasibility

- Examination of business risks and how they will be addressed
- Explanation of any divergence or shortfall that might have occurred in meeting the original business motivation
- Exploration of specific reengineering opportunities
- Acquisition of rapid and highly focused feedback

A page from one recent project's Policy Charter is presented in Figure 2. This segment (which represents about 15 percent of the entire deliverable) is presented in its original computer-automated form. We find graphic presentation (as opposed to a purely textual format) enables better communication and discussion among business-side team members and sponsors.

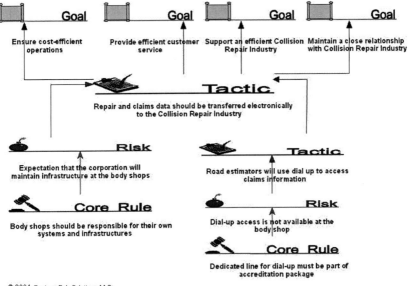

© 2004. Business Rule Solutions, LLC.

Figure 2 - Sample Policy Charter (segment)

This sample Policy Charter segment concerns a business process for handling insurance claims. Reengineering of the business process features automated handheld pads to estimate repair costs for damaged autos. The elements shown in the segment include business goals, tactics, risks, and core business rules linked in appropriate manner. Note the prominent role of core business rules in addressing business risks.

If any element of a draft Policy Charter is unacceptable, unworkable, or incomplete, business sponsors can immediately take appropriate action with minimal loss of time and resources relative to the project as a whole. Such early intervention will be much less costly than during later phases of the project during which technical design, construction, and testing occur.

Our experience is that with the right people and the right approach, a Policy Charter can often be developed in a matter of days. Also, we find that sponsors almost always enjoy their participation in the process. Consider the Policy Charter as an essential step on the road to success with both business processes and business rules.

Conclusion: The Value Proposition of Business Rules

To conclude this chapter's focus on business rules and what they add to business process development, I will summarize the overall value proposition of business rules. The following discussion itemizes key challenges facing businesses today, and the solution offered by the business rules approach.

Ad hoc Rules

Most businesses have no logical approach for defining the business rules associated with their business processes. As a result, business workers often make up the rules as they go along. This leads to confusion, contradiction, and operational inefficiency. After-the-fact resolution of these problems wastes time and resources, and causes frustration for customers and staff alike. The larger the organization, the bigger the problem. Also, since many business rules involve monetary transactions (e.g., should a customer be given a discount, and if so, how much), it can also directly affect the business's bottom line.

Business Rule Solution: A structured approach to help you think through business rules before the fact.

Miscommunication

Misunderstanding of key business concepts inevitably results in miscommunication. Does preferred customer discount mean the same across all departments? If not, what are the differences? What rules apply? Do these rules differ for different business processes? Are the rules consistent?

Business Rule Solution: A clear set of concepts on which business rules (and other specifications) can be directly based.

Inaccessible Rules

Finding out what rules apply to a given business situation often involves an open-ended search through multiple sources. It is common in the end to resort to the application source code. Pursuing rules in this fashion is time-consuming, inefficient and inaccurate.

Business Rule Solution: A means to manage business rules, providing direct accessibility.

Massive Differentiation

Many businesses seek to support highly individualized relationships with growing numbers of customers and other partners for ever more complex product/services. How can businesses massively differentiate between business parties and at the very same time conduct each business transaction faster, more accurately, and at ever lower cost?

Business Rule Solution: A rule-based approach featuring rapid development and deployment of rules.

Keeping Up To Speed

Rapid change, at an ever faster pace, is a fact of life. In the internet age, implementation of changes is expected almost instantaneously. How can line workers consumed with day-to-day activities ever hope to keep up?

Business Rule Solution: Real-time delivery of business logic to knowledge workers as errors actually occur creating a seamless, never-ending, self-training environment.

Knowledge Walking Out the Door

By and large, baby-boomers created much of the operational business capacity and operational systems we see in place in larger organizations today. Much of the related knowledge still sits in their heads – and nowhere else. What will happen when they retire? On a smaller scale, vital operational knowledge walks out the door almost every day. *Business Rule Solution: A systematic way of capturing, documenting and retaining the business rules to ensure the continuing viability of the business processes.*

References.

---

[1] For an independent guide to such platforms, refer to www.brcommunity.com/faqs.php.

[2] This separation is commonly known as Rule Independence. Refer to the Business Rules Manifesto, www.businessrulesgroup.org.

[3] From work on "Organizing Business Strategy: The Standard Model for Business Rule Motivation" [Business Rules Group 2000], Available at www.businessrulesgroup.org

[4] How business rules should be structured and expressed most effectively is beyond the scope of this discussion. However, the fundamentals are well-established. For additional discussion, refer to Parts II and III respectively of Principles of the Business Rule Approach, by Ronald G. Ross, Addison-Wesley, Boston, MA, 2003

[5] RuleSpeakR syntax and guidelines are presented in detail in Part III of Principles of the Business Rule Approach, by Ronald G. Ross, Addison-Wesley, Boston, MA, 2003

[6] I do not mean project goals or project objectives, so to avoid confusion I will continue to say business goal rather than simply goal.

[7] For in-depth discussion, refer to Lam, Gladys S. W. 1998. "Business Knowledge—Packaged in a Policy Charter." Available at www.BRCommunity.com.

Nine

8 Omega

By Steve Towers, David Lyneham-Brown, Terry Schurter and
Mark McGregor

INTRODUCTION: *One of the most challenging issues in BPM is not the question of*
"If" it is the question of "How." In this chapter, the 8 Omega Framework is pre-
sented as the "How" of business process management. Drawing from decades of real
experience with real (and successful) BPM initiatives, 8 Omega is a broad reaching
and flexible framework for taking BPM from promise to practice.

In every organization large or small, the chances are that over time
a plethora of methods and techniques (such as Lean Design, Six Sigma,
Total Quality Management, ISO 9000, Structured Analysis and Design,
etc.) have been used to improve, control, optimize and manage change
within the organization. These practices have yielded great benefit, yet
today businesses are being challenged to determine what practice(s)
should be employed in their organization that will yield ongoing value
while meeting the rigorous demands of external change forces that often
threaten the very existence of the business.

The fact that Business Process Management is currently "in vogue"
has substantial affect on the issue of practice. As companies seek to embrace the concepts of Business Process Management - and more specifically Enterprise Business Process Management - the challenge is no
longer deciding what practice to employ but instead what method to use
for implementation of BPM. This is augmented by the concern of how
to embrace BPM in a non-disruptive way so that we "don't throw out
the baby with the bathwater."

This can be a difficult challenge. All too often the debate on methods and approaches derails the BPM initiative long before an organization has even reached the implementation stage leaving the initiative in

disarray without creating any value to the organization. Experience shows us that there is no "one size fits all" method to ensure a successful BPM project. The varying approaches to BPM all hold substantial merit when correctly applied, however they also have limitations stemming from many environmental factors that have channelled them into a specific direction or to meet a specific application scenario.

This creates a substantial problem in the marketplace as what worked in one scenario may suffer scalability limitations in another, or management buy-in that was relatively simple in one scenario may not be adequately addressed in others hamstringing the entire BPM initiative. Misapplication of resources can also easily occur resulting in creation of internal barriers, flawed modelling, lack of focus and failure to reap benefits.

The scalability issue is driven by a natural tendency to focus methods and approaches on a per project or individual basis. This makes complete sense as up till now most BPM initiatives have been led by consultants or a small number of internal BPM advocates, with most work being applied to a selective subset of business processes. What good does it do to provide a framework for enterprise-wide deployment of BPM if the focus is on tactical ROI projects? The answer is quite simply that it is easier to skip the translation of such a framework to the actions and activities needed for a specific project and jump to an approach that fits neatly into the specific action being taken. However, with BPM adoption now shifting towards enterprise BPM deployment we find the old methods and approaches fail to scale.

The most prominent "resource" having the greatest impact on BPM is people. BPM creates value from the work people do, not from the technology, approach or method being employed. Incorrect use of resource is most often seen when companies notice that a person has "Analyst" in their job title and assume that this skill is generic across all functions, with the ability to blithely move between Systems, Business and Process Analysis. In reality, the skill requirements for these analysis roles are dramatically different with each having specific skills, knowledge and experience needed if they are to be conducted successfully. If required skill sets are not recognized, and appropriately skilled human resources available (or trained) and properly utilized, the "work" within the BPM initiative will fall short of delivering the value intended.

The second example of incorrect use of resource can apply to the method or technique itself. While ISO 9000 and Six Sigma are both process centric approaches the types of problems for which you would use these techniques is completely different. Yet in many organizations it is assumed that one size will fit all.

The most prominent issue is also the most difficult issue to address and the most neglected aspect of BPM. This issue is management "buy-in." A complex issue, management buy-in needs to drive uniformity of purpose, focus and practice down through the organization in direct linkage to strategy. Clearly, when leadership is lacking or mandates are simply dumped on functional area management the entire BPM initiative takes on a piecemeal structure that is reflective of the old issues that have created the dysfunctional silo and island issues we have all learned to fear. For enterprise BPM to succeed – no, for *business process management to create the value it represents*, the initiative must be directly coupled to strategy, and strategy must be directly driven by customer outcomes. It is certainly easier to skip over management buy-in and dive into tactical BPM projects but this will not create any sustainable business transformation.

Remember the saying, "no pain, no gain?" Well, it is painful to change an organization and it does take hard work and dedication to successfully change. However, the benefits to be gained from becoming more customer focused, and using BPM to get there, are too great to let internal issues and politics get in the way of allowing managers to run the business more efficiently.

A Different Perspective

These issues are not something uncovered from research, theorizing or logical deduction. It is the repetitive manifestation of these issues in real BPM initiatives with real corporations that forced them into the light. Like dross on molten metal, these issues rise from BPM activities to cloud the purity of the BPM value underneath.

The realization that these issues were prevalent and consistent triggered the translation of one-off work to the development of a repeatable tool, or framework, for addressing these issues. This was the birth of the

8 Omega Framework. But what is 8 Omega? Another method, approach, opinion or product? No.

What was realized is that implementing BPM is itself a definable business process, one that has steps, order, importance, key elements, conditional routing, common objects, known resources and business rules. The 8 Omega Framework is essentially a business process (more correctly, an enterprise business process) that enforces empirical requirements while providing the flexibility to adapt to the specificity and nuance of each organization's needs and situation. In order to retain the optimal value of 8 Omega the definition is contained at the highest level, avoiding the impulse to drop down into unnecessary strictures that in turn, limits applicability. 8 Omega mandates where necessary to meet empirical needs but retains complete flexibility everywhere else.

8 Omega is not intended to replace the methods and approaches already in use within an organization. It was developed to enable companies to move forward positively and quickly along the BPM road, by harmonising approaches and closing the gaps between the key aspects of the business. 8 Omega can be seen as both a questioning tool and decision tool to enable all stakeholders in an organisation to recognise the current position. From this base point they can then all understand the gaps, act on addressing those gaps and ensure that proposed solutions are complete - tying back to strategy, the addressing of people issues and process, while being supported by appropriate systems.

Understanding the 8 Omega Framework

Having earlier termed the 8 Omega Framework a business process, we can expand this statement by saying that 8 Omega is a business process covering the four key perspectives, or dimensions, of the organization (Strategy, People, Process, Systems) with 8 activity definitions (DADVIICI or Discovery, Analysis, Design, Validate, Integrate, Implement, Control, Improve) applied to all 4 dimensions.

In reality, the 8 Omega Framework is a business process with numerous sub-processes. For those of you who are technically inclined, there is a primary process definition (DADVIICI) that has multiple instances, with each instance having its own sub-processes (which also can have their own instances). For those not technically inclined, 8 Omega is an overall guide with specific guidance at every point where action is required with specific information on what and how to successfully complete each action. This is why it is termed a framework.

When considering 8 Omega, it is very important to realize its intended purpose. 8 Omega is the domain expertise from over a decade of BPM initiatives focused on the highest value of BPM, the transformation of the organization to an adaptive, efficient, agile, innovative and optimized entity that becomes continually evolving. This is best practice BPM, representing the true potential BPM has in creating businesses that are self-sustaining regardless of what external or internal forces are imposed on the business.

But 8 Omega is not a substitute for hard work and dedicated effort. It is work that creates value, not 8 Omega (or the various BPM approaches, sundry methods or technology). These are all tools that can help us choose the right work to perform, and to perform our work in an order that yields the greatest value. 8 Omega is a tool designed to guide, or assist, any organization with the successful adoption of BPM.

It should also be understood that 8 Omega is not a BPM shortcut, it is exactly the opposite. 8 Omega requires a degree of rigour that is often lacking in many BPM approaches. Framework actions are clearly defined with no latitude provided for those wishing to shortcut or skip steps in a rush to "get to results" or to avoid activities that are difficult or uncomfortable. The purpose is to provide the guidance for those who wish to truly transform their organization.

The 8 Omega Framework is also cyclical, meaning that it is not a straight road with a beginning and end. The process of 8 Omega is designed for repetition as an ongoing business process improvement behaviour.

The Framework

As can be seen from the diagram in Figure 1, the 8 Omega Framework is comprised of a vertical axis comprised of Strategy, People, Process and Systems. These are the four dimensions or characteristics of the organization that experience shows us must be included in the BPM plan if we are to achieve our goals. By spanning these four dimensions of the organization, all of the major factors influencing the outcome of

BPM are covered in the framework.

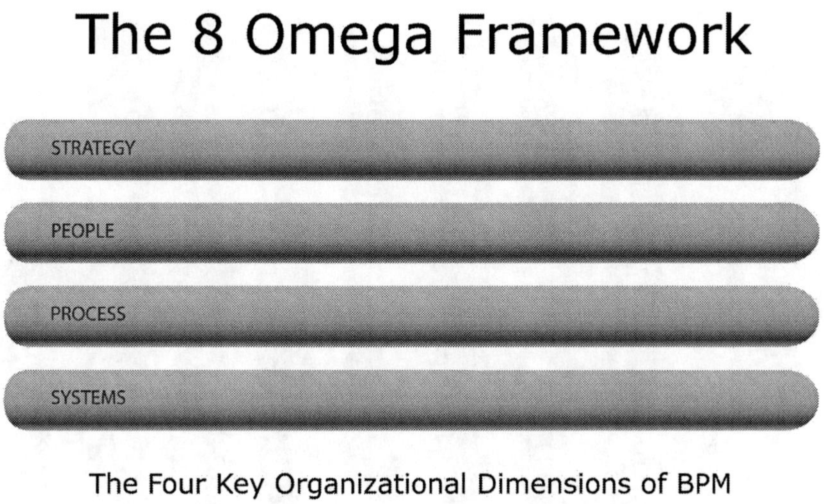

The 8 Omega Framework

STRATEGY

PEOPLE

PROCESS

SYSTEMS

The Four Key Organizational Dimensions of BPM

Figure 1 – 8 Omega Dimensions

The horizontal axis is composed of the activities (or maybe it is better to say the processes) that must be performed in their logical order if we are to maximum the results of business process management. These activities are Discovery, Analysis, Design, Validate, Integrate, Implement, Control and Improve – or DADVIICI – but though they are prescribed activities there is the flexibility for wide variation in the actual activities performed for each activity.

The 8 Omega Framework

The 8 Guiding Activities of the Framework

Figure 2 – 8 Omega Activities

It takes a bit to absorb this comprehensive framework due to its flexibility and "touchy, feely" aspects involving people. Yet the fact is, though many activities can perform regimented or prescribed functions that machines (including computers and software) can do for us, business process management relies heavily on the often fickle and always complex organizational elements of people. People are a fundamental part of every enterprise business process and it is people wherein the greatest opportunity lies.

The 8 Omega Framework

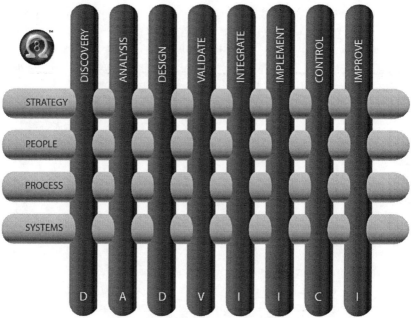

Figure 3 – The 8 Omega Framework

To reinforce this point, and to emphasize the breadth of the 8 Omega Framework, consider these examples of BPM elements that are unconditionally dependent on people.

- Modelling business processes
- Identifying and defining enterprise business processes
- Linking customer outcome strategy with enterprise business processes
- Discovery and analysis relating to improvement of the E-BPMs
- Determining business rules.
- Execution of the plan.

There are of course, many more elements that rely on people. The point is that a viable framework must take into account the pragmatic elements of BPM in conjunction with the people aspect – oh, and don't forget this must be applied across the four dimensions of the organization.

That's what 8 Omega does and the framework goes as deep (or as shallow) as necessary regardless of what the specifics of the situation may be. The goal is to provide the guidance and resources needed for people to succeed in the implementation and ongoing expansion of business process management. The BPM Group provides the framework free to all members of www.bpmg.org while supporting the framework with a broad set of online and classroom training programs.

8 Omega in Practice

The principles of the 8 Omega Framework for Business Process has been successfully applied in many organizations around the globe, across a whole variety of industry sectors. Examples include:

European Insurance Organisation
Struggling with increased competition and regulatory control AXA, the Paris based financial services group with over 50 million customers worldwide embarked on a comprehensive review harmonising strategy, people, process and systems. The process led review of its operations enable AXA to reposition successfully and survive a shakeout which destroyed several of its rivals. The essence of the review involved the co-ordination and subsequent integration of previously discrete approaches to organisation growth and management especially the 'hard wiring' from strategy into the operational front line areas. The new capability "…allows us to be Fast, Fit and Flexible," as one board member states "and this approach is now part of our everyday thinking. It has become a way of life – not a one shot activity."

US Retailing Company
Some organisations have adopted the framework approach as a consequence of 'rules changing' and this is precisely where Levi Strauss, US based apparel manufacturing company, found themselves.

"The balance of power shifted," says Levi Chief Executive Officer Philip Marineau. "When I first started in this business, particularly in

packaged goods, retailers were a way station to the consumer. Manufacturers had a tendency to tell retailers how to do business." With the tables turned, once-mighty brands such as Levi must undergo transformations to put retailers' wishes ahead of their own. When Levi began to sell
to Wal-Mart Stores Inc., it over hauled its enterprise core processes,
from design to production, pricing to distribution, order to fulfilment
and the like. The process was wrenching and full of setbacks, and it is
only now showing signs of paying off. "We had to adopt an approach
that allowed us to change People, Practices and systems," the chief executive says. He adds: "It's been somewhat of a D-Day invasion approach." Regarded as a brilliant strategist from his time at Pepsi
Marineau's focus has been about reversing the $3 billion meltdown
(from about $7 billion in 1995) and building through the strategy, peo-
ple, process and systems a new business model as a consumer-driven
marketing company. The latest results suggest Levi are on track "We're
doing what we said we'd do. We set out to improve our profitability..
and our business is healthier and more competitive today."

Global Financial Services Company

Capital One, established in 1994, is a high growth financial services
company with extensive operations in North America and Europe with
more than $70 billion in managed loans (2004). Successful since its crea-
tion Capital One nevertheless embarked on a customer focused program
through high level process definition (within the overall strategy) and
cascaded this into the training and education of its people. Identifying
the increasing pressure on its margins Capital One utilized its knowledge
and experience in customer acquisition through marketing, "what's in
your wallet" is known the world over, and extending this approach to
full process lifecycle management. Creating the linkage between the high
level strategy, people behaviours, process integration with innovation
and then ensuring the technology delivers on the promise is key to this
success. Capital One now have the lowest acquisition cost of any major
credit card issuer and continue to innovate through this systematic
framework approach.

As can be seen, the 8 Omega Framework can be applied in all sizes of organization, it is not tied to any single methodology and delivers concrete business results. By applying the Framework organizations have found that it can be used to bring together people from all parts of an organization to great effect. Finally in every case where the discipline has been applied organizations have found themselves delivering superior customer service at a lower cost.

The 8 Omega Framework for Business Process has been developed by Steve Towers, David Lyneham-Brown, Terry Schurter and Mark McGregor. It brings together a combined total of over 50 years experience in Business Process. The developers also greatly acknowledge the input and feedback they have received from a number of other leading thinkers in the field including Andrew Spanyi, Roger Burlton, Brad Power, and Tom Davenport. They also recognise the valuable contribution from the numerous clients they have worked with where they have applied the techniques contained in it to great success. Information on the 8 Omega Framework and further reading can be found at (www.bpmg.org).

Ten

BPM and Continuous Improvement

By Jorge Coelho

INTRODUCTION: *In this chapter, Jorge Coelho of SisConsult, discusses the importance of BPM at the center of continuous improvement and the requirements of an effective strategy-oriented intervention methodology needed to support ongoing BPM.*

The purpose of this chapter is to convey the importance of Continuous Business Improvement as an approach to implementing the business's strategy. The idea is to stress the importance of an integrated and systemic approach to the organization, which introduces some new concepts, such as Organizational Therapy and a Business Object approach to BPM.

The objective here is not to improve the processes in themselves, but to implement a new management business model that ensures better performance from a learning organization perspective. Human capital and knowledge management are important features of this Process Intelligence approach.

We present some requirements for an effective methodology, focusing on the way to manage change involving the business's managers. These findings come from practical experience with a variety of organizational types as well as from academic discussions. Finally, we put forward some conclusions.

Requirements of an effective strategy-oriented intervention methodology

The practice around BPM over the last eight years has enabled us to design an eclectic BPM method and to identify some fundamental requirements for a successful implementation of a Continuous Improvement Model geared towards ensuring a more effective implementation of the business strategy.

The requirements are listed below followed by a brief discussion of each point.

- Focus on the strategy and the organization as a whole
- Use an Organizational Therapy approach
- Pay attention to the management of knowledge
- Model the Process-Centric Enterprise Architecture in a systemic and Business Object oriented way
- Deploy the strategy using a Process-Centric Enterprise Architecture
- Define a Continuous Improvement Management Model and the respective implementation team
- Use interactive and real time techniques

Focus on the strategy and the organization as a whole

The business strategy should embrace the entire organization and follow a BPM approach. To ensure effectiveness, every improvement, no matter the subject, must be justified by its contribution to the business strategy and goals. Thus, before initiating any project, one needs to clearly understand the orientations to the project, starting from the organization's strategy and its business improvement objectives. Further, it is important to know the processes that belong to the scope of the project and the place of these processes in the enterprise architecture.

If there is no enterprise architecture already modelled, there are two ways to progress. The best way is to create the conditions to do the modelling, in a top down fashion, at least until it is possible to define the context of the processes to improve: namely their interfaces. When a top down approach is not possible, one should use a *middle down* version.

To implement a middle-down approach we need to define at least a rough picture of the first level of processes in order to ensure a minimum degree of integration. Then, we drill down to the level where we find all the processes to be analysed and improved. All the interfaces should be clearly defined between the target process and its context. The process context is the set of processes and external entities with which the process establishes relevant relationships.

To get the improvement to the whole organization one needs to define the contribution of each process. This contribution should be expressed in terms of the objectives and goals of the process. Then we define a project and establish the goals for the project according to the goals defined for all target processes.

This approach means that one can not develop organizational improvements by function or department. If the board of a company decides to improve the organization of a certain department, it is wrong to identify the AS IS situation, to model the processes and then to analyse them. The right approach is to identify primarily the target processes in the enterprise architecture. So the negative practices we normally see (that must be addresses in our efforts) can be summarized as follows:

- Improving processes without defining the process context in the enterprise architecture.

- Defining project goals according directly from the strategy, without linking these to processes objectives and goals alignment.

- Applying a BPM approach restricted to a departmental area.

Use an Organizational Therapy approach

Most BPM approaches are based on an "AS IS" characterization of the organization and of the processes.[1] After collecting all the information, the analysts initiate the analysis of the processes.

We must stress that the main objective of our approach is to create better conditions to implement the business's strategy in a more effective way. Thus, the most fundamental factor is people, and if we do not change the mindset of those involved it will not be possible to improve the processes and, of course, the organization. If each person in the company has his/her own view of the organization it is difficult to have effective communication and a convergent decision process.

Normally, it is difficult to find a company where all its employees have the some picture of the organization. This stems from the fact that the organizational chart only says who manages who and what but not what is done and how. A good way to solve this is to design an enterprise architecture, so that the organizational picture is unique.[2] In this case, it is important to ensure that the architecture really represents the strategy and that it is well understood by everybody.

This means that the purpose of each workshop should not be only to discover and capture information but also to contribute to the building of a unique picture of the organization.

When running the workshops it is important to ensure that everything is discussed and consensus is achieved. At the end of each session the board and business managers should know more about the organization than they did before the session. They should be surprised with the findings. People often discover that they have different views and understandings of the strategy and of the organization, although they had thought differently for years.

During the workshops it is difficult for each participant to withhold information, to give the wrong information, to defend their own (or their department's) interests. Also, given that the discussion is strategy-oriented, participants should not be concerned with functions, departments or "AS IS" methods.

In many cases, managers say that they consider the results logical and consistent but that they cannot agree. However, at the same time, they don't know how to disagree. This leads to an impasse where effective communication and problem solving cannot be achieved. That is why we call this approach an Organizational Therapy. The workshops offer the opportunity to rethink the organization, crossing different views and building consensus horizontally. There are no individual interviews at this stage. This stage (design of the enterprise architecture until activities level) should be done within a period of one or two months. So the negative practices we normally see (that must be addresses in our efforts) can be summarized as follows:

- Process improvement is focused on methods and tools improvement, forgetting sometimes the people dimension,

- BPM approach begins with an "AS IS" analysis,

- The role of the business people is focused in the transfer of information for the team project and not in provoking a rethinking of the organization,

- The approach is only based on individual interviews,
- The task of documenting methods and procedures is too heavy, making it difficult to run the workshops and interviews with enthusiasm on the part of business people.

Pay attention to the management of knowledge

To implement the business strategy in an effective way, the organization needs to reuse the knowledge coming from experience. Knowledge management is thus an important issue in BPM approaches. It deals with explicit and tacit knowledge. The former calls for the creation of an organizational repository and the latter draws attention to the management of Human Capital.

A large barrier to the creation of an organizational repository is the enormous amount of work required to build and maintain it. This happens because normally the analysts gather information from interviews or workshops then they systematize the information and come back to the business people in order to validate the final document. Only then do they arrange all information in a repository.

The only way to succeed in creating and maintaining an organizational repository is to base its creation on interactive methods. Thus, the creation and the maintenance of the repository are carried out at the same time, while running the workshops or the interviews. This way all the information is validated in real time by all the participants. Once created, the repository should be maintained by business people, namely the process team of each process. The repository should be for everyone in the organization.

Another problem deals with the lack of integration of the repository. As discussed earlier, this is eliminated if there is only one repository supporting the enterprise architecture, and not one repository per department. So the negative practices we normally see (that must be addresses in our efforts) can be summarized as follows:

- Existence of an organizational repository.
- Build the repository not in real time with business people.
- The repository is not integrated.
- The repository is not maintained by business people.

Model the business architecture in a systemic and business object-oriented way

We have already talked about the importance of process centric enterprise architecture to support business strategy. Process centric enterprise architecture has the ability to be better understood by business people and to be considered a useful management tool.

Enterprise architecture is very important in a BPM approach. It is the bridge between the strategy and the bottom level and has the following uses:

- It helps the conveying of consensus about the unique picture of the organization, as discussed in requirement 2
- It supports the deployment of the strategy, according to the different decisions levels, also as discussed in requirement 2. This will be discussed further in requirement 5
- It clarifies the responsibilities of everybody in the organization, enabling the definition of collaborative objectives instead of shared ones
- It defines a framework from which to analyse the "AS IS" situation of each process.

To build an enterprise architecture, one must pay attention to the method and to the way the method is used. First of all it's essential to separate two important stages. The first is related to the layers of processes down to the activity level. The second corresponds to the "AS IS" characterization at the task level. We consider the hierarchy of several layers of processes. The lowest level process has two layers: the activity and the task level. Each task is a group of operations or procedures.

The first stage is based on workshops and it represents a rethinking of the organization (as previously discussed). It is the opportunity to reach consensus about a unique and corporate-wide view of the organization. During this stage we capture the culture and the DNA of the organization. The only ingredients should be the organization's mission, its strategy, its stakeholders and its business managers, including the board of directors. This is a crucial stage in all BPM approaches and it is here that one can differentiate one BPM method from the next.

The first levels of the architecture should be defined in a workshop where the board or its representatives should participate. It should not take more than half a day. The remaining levels should be defined in separate workshops, with the selected managers, in accordance with the target processes and their contexts. Each workshop should take between two and four hours, depending on the process complexity.

In order to discover and define the processes, one needs a method that uses objective criteria. It is important to understand that the processes are already in place. The task is not to define but to discover the processes. So, the criteria should be the same for the whole company. If the criteria are not objective, then there will be many difficulties in achieving consensus and the results are likely to be inconsistent.

Our experience with a business object-oriented method has been quite successful. We consider a process as a capability to respond to a stimulus coming from an external entity or another process. At the same time, a process is associated to the life cycle of one or more business objects.

A Business Object is an entity that gathers all the information needed to respond to a stimulus. We give it the same name of the respective stimulus. For example, consider the case of a client ordering an article. When the company receives the order we say that it is receiving a stimulus which we call Client Order. Then, we create a capability to respond to the stimulus and we call it a Process named Client Order Management. Associated with the stimulus we create a Business Object named Client Order. In this way, the process is defined in terms of business objects. The beginning and the end of the process is defined in terms of status of the business object.

According to the stimuli from stakeholders we discover the first level of processes. Then we decompose the processes according to the number of business objects. When we reach a level where a process has only one business object we stop. We call it an elementary business process. Next step is the decomposition of the process into activities. An activity is a set of tasks needed to manage a control point in a process. So, according to the required control points, we are able to define the activities. This technique enables the clarification of responsibilities at all levels in the organization.

The second stage can now go ahead. The "AS IS" characterization is done based on interviews or workshops but always oriented by the framework build during the first stage. Thus it is possible to define the scope and to select the information to be gathered. This accelerates the entire project.

We stress that the "TO BE" model relates only to the task level. The upper levels, done during the first stage, only change when the strategy changes. Another important benefit is that in the end training is not required for managers and middle-management in order to deal with or for updating the enterprise architecture. Because they were all involved in its construction, they are all already well acquainted with the architecture. So the negative practices we normally see (that must be addresses in our efforts) can be summarized as follows:

- Inexistence of an objective criteria to define a process and its decomposition

- The building up of the enterprise architecture starting from the "AS IS" situation

- The adoption of templates and good practices without rethink the organization, in order to get a unique, corporate-wide picture of the organization

- The use of IT-centric, instead of process-centric enterprise architectures

- Designing the architecture for the board and not with the board

- Taking too long to deliver the enterprise architecture

Deploy the strategy using a Process-Centric Enterprise Architecture

Nowadays the Balanced Scorecard is being used in most organizations as the method to deploy the strategy. In spite of the excellent contributions it has offered, there are some problems with its application. These problems, or limitations, are as follows:

- The subjectivity associated with building of the strategic maps.

- The fact that it is too focused on the client, with little discussion regarding the other stakeholders.

- The absence of a process approach.

- The definition of shared objectives, making it difficult to ascertain individual responsibilities.
- The absence of a stage in the methodology to reach consensus about the actual situation and before moving on to the definition of objectives and measures.

With a business object-oriented enterprise architecture, these problems can be solved. As the processes are defined in a client-supplier relationship, it is easy to define the objectives for each client. The objectives are then defined in a mutually exclusive way and are not shared. All the stakeholders are analyzed using the context model of the organization. This is done to support the identification of the first level of processes.

Before defining the objectives, the architecture building process allows the organization to reach consensus about the actual situation. The idea is to identify the issues raised by the analyses of stakeholders' relationships. The issues are considered as unfulfilled responses to the stimuli. This analysis is carried out in a workshop organized with the top level of the organization.

The strategic maps will be obtained by using the decision levels of the architecture. For each process, the same method as explained above is used, changing the workshop participants in accordance with the context of the process under review.

Each manager gets the objectives and goals associated with the processes that have been put under his/her responsibility. The method does not allow objectives and goals to be attributed directly to positions on the organizational chart! We need to stress that all the measures are based on a Business Object status, as they represent control points in the processes. So the negative practices we normally see (that must be addresses in our efforts) can be summarized as follows:

- The subjectivity associated with the definition of objectives, in methods such as the BSC.
- Definition of objectives not based on control points in the processes.
- Definition of shared objectives, making it difficult to ascertain individual responsibilities.
- Absence of a stage in the methodology to reach consensus about the

actual situation and before moving on to the definition of objectives and measures.

- Process objectives are not the same used by the management control, neither the ones used by human resources management to support the staff appraisals or compensation definition.

Define a Continuous Improvement Management Model and the respective implementation team

Our approach is moulded on a learning organization or continuous improvement paradigm. This means, among other things, that everyone in the organization should have access to the same organizational repository. The repository should be used to support the quality manual, the definition of information requirements, the definition of training needs, the deployment of strategy, BPM modelling, operational risk management and to help express evidence to comply with all the norms and regulations that apply to the organization.

The repository should be used whenever anyone is rethinking the organization. It should not be used only to store information about the organization but to support the communication and to reinforce a unique organization view. One important factor in this design is the team that is responsible for the management of the continuous improvement effort.

It is also important to reconcile the process architecture with the organization's structure, as represented in its organizational chart. The process manager should be someone with a position in the organizational chart of the business. In addition, the process manager should have a process coordinator, to help in the process improvement role.

If a process crosses two departments, then there should be two process managers, but only one process coordinator. All the improvements suggested by this process coordinator should be approved by both process managers. Thus, the continuous improvement team should be based on the board, process managers, process coordinators, management control, human resources and IT managers. So the negative practices we normally see (that must be addresses in our efforts) can be summarized as follows:

- The continuous improvement is of the responsibility of a central team, not involving the process manager.
- The improvement of the process is of the responsibility of a process owner without any authority in the organizational chart.
- The improvements are not supported by an organizational repository.
- The continuous improvement is dispersed inside the organization through the TQM team, the BPM team, the IT team and others.
- The improvements are not strategy-oriented.

Use interactive and real time techniques

All techniques recommended in our approach are based on the notion of sharing and validation of the information gathered, in real time. At least spreadsheets, word processors or drawing tools should be use as supporting devices.

All workshops and interviews should be supported by an appropriate software tool, so that the information gathering exercise (i.e. the workshops) can be quickly understood by the participants, validated and shared, in real-time. This is a critical success factor in order to accelerate BPM approaches, foster the participation of business managers and maintain the organizational repository updated. So the negative practices we normally see (that must be addresses in our efforts) can be summarized as follows:

- The use of paper to support workshops and interviews.
- The use of too structured software tools, making the flow of the workshops cumbersome and slow.
- The use of several, not integrated, software tools.

Conclusion

To sum up we will say that it is not an easy task to apply a BPM approach. To add real value to the business, the approach should be top down, systemic, integrated, strategy oriented and use a process-centric enterprise architecture. A business object orientation reduces subjectivity and accelerate consensus.

It is very important to follow a method, but much more important is the way you apply it. It should be people oriented and in a context of organizational therapy. One should establish a continuous improvement management model to ensure the progress of the business improvement.

Finally, attention should be given to the software tools used to speed up the information-gathering exercise as well as to motivate people as active participants.

Note: The author would like to recognize the thoughts and insights of Paul Harmon (BP Trends) as influential in the development of the material presented herein.

References.

[1] Laury Verner, The Challenge of Process Discovery, white paper CTO, ProActivity Inc., May 2004

[2] Richard D. Buchanan, Richard Mark Soley, Aligning Enterprise Architecture and IT Investments With Corporate Goals, January 2003.

Eleven

BPM Software: Why you Need it and how to Maximize its Value

By Terry Schurter

INTRODUCTION: *In this chapter, Terry Schurter, BPM Group Chief Analyst, turns a critical eye onto BPM software in presenting the rational behind the need for BPM software and the important (and often overlooked) critical points that must be considered to maximize the value of BPM software.*

In looking at the majority of information from thought leaders and analysts regarding business process management, the message that comes through loud and clear is that BPM is organizational behavior and business practice more than it is a product.

This is true, but if it is, then why are there so many business process management software products and companies out there? The BPM product market is booming, a veritable who's who list of enterprise software vendors and emerging software concerns (further resources on BPM products and vendors are available at www.bpmg.org). Why does the primary discussion not center on these products rather than this behavior and practice focus?

It's simple really, for BPM is the center of a long-term business evolution and leading experts understand that the communication of the BPM "big picture" can easily be lost if discussions drop too quickly into a product focus. The concern is that BPM will be implemented in a very narrow, tactical manner, which not only misses the point but can easily translate into BPM software deployment that actually limits the ability of the organization to evolve through its myopic design approach.

This is certainly a valid concern but it is also true that a substantial number of IT executives and system designers have developed a reasonable understanding of the longer term BPM view. For these people, BPM software deployment is not myopic and there is little concern that implementation will box the business into a dead-end technology corner somewhere down the road.

In addition, the reasons for implementing BPM are growing rapidly (including the capabilities, functions and maturities of BPM products) and are actually expanding in ways that many IT decision makers have not yet considered. There is also a very big concern that other IT technologies and quasi-BPM approaches will be implemented (many are now on IT budgets) that will confuse, complicate and otherwise weaken the ability of the organization to implement BPM to its fullest advantage.

Further, there are reasons to implement BPM as *the* initial step in organizational pursuit of BPM. That's right, there are valid approaches to flipping the table (albeit with a certain degree of risk) and implementing BPM without executive buy-in on organizational transformation or even agreement that the business needs to be viewed from the perspective of business processes.

The reasons to implement BPM are so compelling that it is hard to understand why BPM software is not on every IT budget "hot list" this year in the preemptive position of "the one thing we must do." A bold statement, perhaps, but here are the reasons why.

Reason One – Building for the Future

Because BPM is an ongoing business evolution, the sooner we have a system in place, the quicker we can become proficient in its use and begin assembling the building blocks we need for the many issues this software will be essential in helping us address as we move through the upcoming cycles of business evolution.

This is the least obvious and direct reason to deploy BPM, as it assumes that we understand some of what is coming in this evolution and believe that this evolution is real. Even when we do understand and believe, this is a point that can be difficult to gain executive consensus on and we all know that the mantra of executive decision making is "if we aren't sure, wait." It is important to make note of this reason, even though it is unlikely to be the rationale that motivates us to push BPM software onto our budgets.

As an interesting side note, although "building for the future" is seen to be a weak justification for the implementation of BPM software right now, we will come back to it later on and see how building for the future actually becomes very compelling once we have a complete picture of what we should be using BPM software for in our organization.

Reason Two – Tactical ROI

Tactical ROI from improvement of selected business processes is still the number one reason why BPM software is purchased. We are a low-hanging fruit, quarterly performance driven society and tactical ROI produces short term affects where all other activities in BPM are a much longer time cycle.

There is also the issue of regulatory and compliance requirements that is imposed on the organization by government agencies and business partners. Because many of these requirements have a very discrete definition, pre-packaged process capability to meet this requirements can be a core tactical benefit. Many BPM software vendors offer support for common processes of this type as part of their product portfolio.

Though tactical ROI may be the most obvious benefit of BPM software, the analytical assessment of tactical ROI provides us with the most important clue to understanding why the other reasons for implementing BPM are even more important – and they are very, very important. "We are a low-hanging fruit, quarterly performance driven society and tactical ROI produces short term affects where *all other activities in BPM are a much longer time cycle*" is the statement that opens the door to insight.

Because the other benefits of BPM software (and BPM) are longer time cycles, and because we *know* that BPM (sum total) value is integral to competitive advantages, then the connection here is that for those businesses that adopt BPM today, versus those that don't, competitive advantages gained will automatically inherent this time duration and so the competitive advantages will also have a minimum known duration before any adequate response can be made from competitors that have not implemented BPM.

In Search of BPM Excellence

In simpler terms, if our competitors invest now in BPM and in 18 or 24 months this investment creates real competitive advantage (and in many, many cases it absolutely will) then we are 18 to 24 months behind them in sustaining our competitive position. Oh, and what do you expect they will do in that 18 to 24 months (or whatever the duration is) that we are scurrying to play catch up? They will most likely be pushing the bar out in front of us again.

This is the most important point we must derive regarding analysis of BPM and when we should deploy BPM software.

Reason Three – Justification for BPM

It is very likely that this reason for implementing BPM software is currently *not* part of the decision making process for most organizations – and at a glance it seems to even be refuting itself. How can it be that we implement BPM software in order to justify the adoption of BPM?

Yet the point holds true when we take the time to work through the logic behind this reason. Now, for starters it is necessary to review some of the basic principles of BPM software. In all cases, there exists the ability either to model the business processes of the organization or to import these models into the BPM software. These process models include the concept of workflow, of actions that occur in each step of the workflow of the modeled processes and often include sub-processes that support higher level processes.

This is a relational model, meaning that once process models are created or imported into the BPM software many of the important relationships of the processes of the organization exist with clear, programmatic relationships in the BPM software. This is not abstract in any way. The relationships are known and a wide variety of actions can be taken in regards to these relationships. This relational model can even be extended to be a master meta-data model of the entire organization.

It is also the case that the majority of organizations are not yet managing from the process perspective (or at least not on the enterprise business process perspective), with management still primarily operating in a functional mode. As a brief recap, remember that enterprise business processes are those processes that span the organization horizontally and that have a customer outcome as their direct output.

Regardless of the accuracy of the enterprise business processes (they will have a reasonable degree of accuracy if generated by anyone that is at least reasonably up on the overall concept of BPM), when enterprise business processes are modeled in BPM software with their supporting business processes and sub-processes the BPM software will give us programmatic informational views (information) about our operations that are likely to provide the justification for, and human motivation to, buy-in to the concept of BPM.

Let's present this a slightly different way. From the enterprise process perspective (without BPM software) we cannot have clear and accurate information regarding where bottlenecks are, what all of the elements are that affect customer outcomes in regards to things like price, accuracy, quality, time, etc. We know some of these things and we suspect others, but without BPM software, we are relegated to a partial picture. The information is simply not available at the level of detail, accuracy, relationship and timeliness for us to really know – and if it is, it has been pieced together in such a way that the data accuracy and critical data relationships are subject to error at numerous points – therefore creating a high degree of risk. As we have all learned, our decision-making ability is only as good as the data we have to make our decisions from and bad data in produces bad decisions out.

In this respect, BPM software can be our means to discover what we need to know for clear justification in taking tactical and strategic BPM actions in our organization. Remember, it is very difficult for executives to make decisions with incomplete information. The risk is great and virtually every seasoned exec has been burned at least once by the promise of a business opportunity or technology investment that failed to produce any real business value. So there is also the issue of visibility, i.e. prior to BPM software implementation it is very difficult to clearly show what the end result will be and we place executives in the position of making decisions based on faith.

Put the enterprise business processes into BPM software as nothing more than a monitoring application and the information from this application will provide all that is needed to support the case for the organization to take aggressive moves on real business process management activities.

Tie this in with one or more low-hanging tactical opportunities and the BPM software yields real ROI - while building the information case to take on more aggressive BPM activities.

Reason Four - SOA

This may also come as a surprise or eye-opener to many, but businesses desiring to migrate their IT infrastructure to a Service Oriented Architecture (SOA) should look to BPM software first. To help in working through the idea of using BPM software for the SOA needs of the organization, let's first review the purpose and goal of SOA.

In simplest terms (and there are many, many expanded definitions), a SOA can be thought of as the software architecture that provides the means to easily plug and play any number of services, including services available over the internet from external parties, into our business systems without substantial programming or other effort.

On a more advanced scale, we see that numerous SOA definitions include service behavior as part of the SOA. In this case, there is a clearly defined process that each service is subject to as part of the SOA, giving us a standardized way for these services to interact with our business systems.

What a SOA needs to do to create business value is to provide a standardized interface into the business, one that is loosely coupled (the plug and play concept) and it needs to provide a means for service processing that can be applied across the entire breadth of the business. And, it needs to have a means for managing the connection points and workflow of all these great services the business uses – and the means to handle all of the non-SOA services that we are using now, many of which are not loosely-coupled and that do not follow the SOA service process.

Did you get that last part? How many SOA proponents even mention these non-SOA requirements? What magic is supposed to happen that suddenly makes every internal and external service SOA compliant (whatever SOA compliant means)?

The fact is that getting to the point where a solid SOA is in place and fully operational with the resources and capabilities available to handle the current state of information systems is best achieved through a business process management system. *That's right, if you really want a*

SOA you need BPM software.

Striking deeper into the logic behind this conclusion expands the definition of the SOA that organizations really need, and that drives the SOA into BPM software. For starters, there is the whole concept of services, which are in many cases business processes or at least processes. As we extend our view of this plug and play service concept, it becomes much easier to assemble the big picture if we start by thinking about our business as a series of enterprise business processes that are further supported by business processes and processes.

Now with BPM software, it is very easy to build a generic SOA process and a generic SOA interface (with whatever standard or standards we choose to support) that can be applied at every interface point. Build it once (or in many cases use existing tools the BPMS vendor includes in their product specifically to handle this) and use it everywhere.

Further, in this approach we have now set aside the SOA service process and interface such that it can be easily changed globally. Gee, that might be nice when the service standards change from XML, to SOAP, to REST, to whatever.

Oh, and what about the service process? What happens if it changes, new processing rules need to be applied or additional functions are desired? Again, change the service process in one place and the changes are globally applied (and can even be controlled through versioning for incremental change). And, BPM software has all of the tools needed to perform custom integration to applications or services that do not yet comply with our SOA structure. Of course, because these interfaces are clearly identified in the process model when they do change to SOA compliant it is a simple matter to switch them over.

Finally, by using BPM software we also gain all of the management tools, optimization capabilities, and automated monitoring and discovery to help us manage and improve our SOA consistently throughout the organization. In contrast, many SOA initiatives will focus on the interfaces and service processes without a clearly evolved underlying architecture to enforce quality, consistency and that enable ongoing adaptation and system management.

Reason Five – Business Survival

Reason one, *Building for the Future,* was introduced as the least compelling reason to use BPM software with the caveat that we would revisit this point later on. Well, that time is now and it is all about business survival. Taken piecemeal, the reasons listed here in support of BPM software are certainly very compelling but hardly represent the core issue of business survival. Yet like pieces of a jigsaw puzzle, once properly assembled a complete and often breathtaking picture emerges.

So it is with BPM software:

- When looking at a business that is paring costs and inefficiencies out of existing processes, building new levels of insight into the business from an information structure we have not had before, beginning to discover numerous opportunities for improvement and optimization that may or may not have even be suspected before...

- When we have an SOA that decouples all of our processes and services from a constrictive integration scenario into a loosely coupled structure enabling "plug and play" of services and processes, outsourcing, in-sourcing – even combination sourcing...

- As our understanding of the business, our processes, process dependencies, and process and data relationships become clearly defined so that we can make broad scale changes based on an accurate understanding of what is, and what we need to do to make "what is" into something different, without risk or undo investment...

- Even as new change comes trouncing down on us, requiring us to include human interaction models in our processes while further extending our business to partners all over the globe as the business collapses into its core competency even further – dramatically expanding outsourcing – and increasing customers, revenue and growth...

- And the other changes we will need to make in the way we do business and with technology that we can't see yet and can't make any specific plans for because we *don't know*...

Then it's clear that having BPM software at the center of our IT infrastructure will be absolutely critical to the very survival of our business.

The fundamental flexibility of BPM software, the very nature of the design of business process management software (and yes, most BPM vendors do understand this fundamental requirement of BPM and they do support this requirement quite well), can not only be adapted to these changes but will help us to make these changes in our business and with our people. These reasons clearly place BPM software front and center on the IT action list.

Part II – How to Maximize BPM software Value

The next most important question is how to maximize the value of BPM software. There are many minor points that are reflective of the specifics of each organization's situation but there are major points that have the greatest affect on value from BPM software that apply to all organizations.

The main activity is the evaluation of what business process management functions are important in each given situation. There are eight major functions to consider.

Prior to jumping into this evaluation though, there is a fundamental design mentality that is essential to the overall value proposition of BPM software. It should be noted, however, that BPM software has consistently been deployed, without this mentality, with stellar ROI results. This does not invalidate the importance of approaching BPM implementation from this perspective. It is more of a weather gauge of the depth of opportunity that really exists with BPM software.

The most important thing to do with BPM software is to build out the basic enterprise business processes in regards to customer outcomes. It is not a difficult task to align this with SOA and tactical activities. It is even best to build the enterprise process model before addressing tactical projects or SOA deliverables because in all cases these actions will have a natural fit in the enterprise process model.

It is entirely acceptable to limit the controlling aspect of the enterprise process model initially. The most important benefit of having the model in place is the information (which will lead to opportunity discovery) that will be available from BPM software with the model in place. This will also provide incredible visibility into the inner workings of the business. It is not an assumption but a guarantee that this information will expand the understanding of the business to an entirely new level of clarity. It will also expand and clarify how to maximize results from tactical opportunities and service orientation. Finally, it will place a wealth of relational capability at the doorstep of optimization and performance improvement.

Remember, when enterprise business processes are modeled and tracked by the BPM engine, we have effectively created the relational model of the enterprise. The mining of this relational model is perhaps more important than any other BPM software benefit. Note that, in some cases there will be multiple BPM software products in use by a given organization. This is fine; however, there *must* be one (and only one) BPM software system that is the master of the enterprise relational model if the full benefits of BPM software are to be realized.

Workflow Process Modeling

Workflow modeling differs from strategic modeling in that the workflow model is a production model and will be acted on by the BPM process engine. Again, there is crossover in the area of strategic modeling and workflow modeling among BPM products.

Selection of the appropriate BPM software is critical regarding the workflow modeling function. This may not seem obvious at first, and the definition of workflow modeling is at best cloudy these days, but here are the questions to ask.

- How many people will be building out the model?
- How complex is our business?
- What is the level of detail we need to drive to in the visual aspect of the model?
- If our model is complex, do we need an engineering style model that our professional process experts can develop and manage?
- Or is the information we need for the model scattered among pockets of domain knowledge throughout our organization?

These are important questions. For complex engineering type modeling, the advanced capabilities of a visual modeling environment will be needed. But what if the model is relatively simple and straightforward?

In this case, a streamlined graphically intuitive modeling environment may be the best choice.

Other cases are simply to complex for composite visual modeling and often have process knowledge and business rule knowledge residing with a diverse group of people in the organization. In these cases, products that have intelligent capabilities to extract this knowledge out of expert resources and into the process model automatically are of particular interest.

The key? Make sure the BPM software workflow modeling environment is a good fit for how you expect to perform workflow modeling, and that you won't get backed into a corner as you expand the process model later.

Automated Optimization and Analysis

There are many advanced and intelligent features available in the BPM products on the market. Many of these functions cannot be performed with any consistency or accuracy by people, so the use of BPM software is a requirement for these functions.

For example, some products have the capability to automatically identify decision elements and present them first, a function that dramatically reduces wasted data entry time (performance improvement) while negating the need (and maintenance) of manual prioritization.

Another example is the monitoring of system behaviors for exceptions, issues and *change*. In BPM software there are many business rules, steps and conditional routing in even the simplest process model. Change often occurs due to some unforeseen circumstance of which there is an infinite set of variations. This is impossible for people to track in any semblance of real-time. Yet BPM software can do just that for us and many BPM products have advanced automated analysis and optimization identification that will present information such as: What is different today? What exception rules are firing often? What rules are not firing? Have queue patterns changed? Is timing within the process different than it was, and why? What is the most significant factor affecting key metrics of each process? What are all of the factors ranked by degree of affect? Many BPM software vendors have strong features in this category.

The Key? Build a set of natural language statements of all things you want to know. Make sure the list is idealistic, as you may be surprised at what BPM software is capable of presenting. Use the list in evaluation of BPM software. Work with BPM vendors to have them show you how their software can present this information to you and how to best use the system to get the most information possible!

Process Metric Model

What is the process metric model? Metric in this case means "a system of measurement" so the expanded definition is *the process model system of measurement*. Taking one more step, this refers to the combination of modeling and software functionality that can capture and present measures by relationship as established by the model created in the workflow modeling environment.

What this means is that because relationships exist as soon as we create process models (most importantly the relationships of enterprise processes, business processes, processes and sub-processes as hierarchical) the opportunity exists for automatic extraction of a wide swath of information relating to each top level measure.

For example, if we measure how long it takes to process an order this measurement is a top level measure of an enterprise process. However, the order process can consist of multiple business processes, processes and sub-processes. How is the process order time sliced up in this process pie? What lies at the bottom of the 3% of exceptions that occur? Do they come from the same place? The same set of conditions?

Make sure to ask BPM vendors what they offer to support the process metric model and what, if any, actions are required by you when preparing your workflow model. BPM vendors by and large will jump at the chance to help you use their software to your fullest advantage and to exploit the full power of the software they have developed. Many of the BPM software product offerings stem from advanced data handling histories, and have a comprehensive set of features and functions to support the process metric model.

The key? Discuss the process metric model with BPM vendors and have them work with you to ensure you are able to capitalize on this critical BPM benefit.

Application Integration

Virtually every BPM product that provides workflow functions includes a broad range of application integration capabilities. There is little chance that integration needs will not be met by the BPM products reviewed. But BPM vendors do not all approach integration in the same manner. It is best to document all of the probable (even possible) applications that may require integration in the BPM software as processes are brought under BPM software control. This document should be presented to each BPM vendor as part of the software evaluation as they will gladly tell you just how they deal with each of these scenarios and what options exist that you may wish to consider.

However, what is really important is to also have BPM vendors address informational only integration for these applications. In many cases at early stages in process model development, what is needed is simply the extraction of certain information from these other applications. The information that needs to be extracted is the information needed to support the overall analysis of the enterprise and processes in the enterprise. In most cases this "loosely coupled" integration has been greatly simplified already by the BPM vendors.

The Key? Prepare a master list of applications that may require integration into the BPM system. Work with the BPM vendor to address both transactional integration requirement and (even more importantly) informational integration requirements.

Real-time Analysis

When process models are fleshed out in BPM software, a vast resource of information that can help in the day to day management of the business becomes available to us. Things change, and sometimes problems pop-up that are often completely unexpected. We often choose to order our work priorities based on the information we have available, as we know what is most important. The issue is one of information, not priority, yet it is seldom the case that we truly have the information we need to make the best choices.

BPMS offers a combination of information and presentation options that is a boon to daily management activities. With visibility into where work is, what bottlenecks exist *right now*, any exceptions that may have occurred, or other events of importance included in the process model design, the daily operational management of the business becomes highly focused on the most important activities.

This visibility reduces response time, often preempting situations that if not responded to quickly enough can balloon into major business issues. It also reduces the time spent in trying to gain the visibility into the business we need to discover issues that need to be addressed. The viable premise behind the capabilities of real-time analysis with BPM software is that all problems can be recognized and dealt with before they can create an accumulative impact on the organization. With this type of information at our fingertips, by the time anyone else recognizes a problem exists – it is already fixed (although in most cases issues are identified so quickly that resolution is in place before the issue can percolate up to a visible level).

The Key? Realize that value of real-time analysis with BPM software, include this analysis in your vendor review and take advantage of these capabilities when you deploy BPM software.

Optimization Analysis

In most cases, when we think of optimization in the context of BPM we think of the optimization of business processes as an activity conducted by people. This is certainly the case, however there are other optimization opportunities specific to BPM software.

For example, consider the behavior of an enterprise business process that is time critical in order to meet customer expectations. With the process properly designed by people, there are major improvements in the critical measure of process time. Yet in many cases, there are numerous details affecting the overall process that we are simply not aware of in our human analysis of the process.

With BPM software, the information and relationships exist to give us insight into all of these details. We can quickly spot trends that affect key metrics, both good and bad, changes that have occurred impacting the behavior of the process and non-conforming behavior.

I would call this fine tuning the enterprise processes, but don't be lulled into believing the gains here are minor. Optimization discovery with BPM software often has a substantial affect on key metrics and competitive advantages!

This optimization also leads us to correcting mistaken assumptions. If the behavior we believe is correct for a given process is not correct (and this will always be the case to at least a minor extent), advanced features and functions of BPM software will lead us to these variances. As with most things, once we *know* an issue exists and have the *specifics* of the issue – the fix becomes nothing more than a task.

The range of optimization features available from BPM software vendors is extremely diverse and should be reviewed against the specific context of each situation. Some vendors have taken this concept along way in trying to make optimization discovery as sweeping as possible.

The Key? Include the subject of optimization as an integral part of vendor discussions. When optimization capabilities are connected to the specifics of an organization's situation and requirements, the value of optimization moves from abstract to very concrete.

Strategic Process Modeling

Strategic process modeling, more commonly termed enterprise modeling, is the most misunderstood function of BPM software and the least supported function in the BPM market. Strategic process modeling is the detailed modeling of enterprise business processes including resource usage and resource consumption.

The purpose of strategic process modeling is to build the enterprise model in software that can analyze the operation of the enterprise, often on a scale that includes all of the enterprise business processes in the business.

For businesses that desire to perform this front-end analysis and design, BPM software must be reviewed for this capability. Many BPM products have little, if any, of this type of capability and it is likely that an enterprise modeling product will be required to meet these needs. Some products are specifically designed to handle true strategic process modeling.

The Key? Determine if Strategic Process Modeling is needed for your organization. If so, select a BPM product that has this capability.

Strategic Model Validation

With the enterprise process model in place, "what if" scenarios can be tested on a broad scale yielding predictive results that show us what affect these changes will have on key metrics, where conflicts may exist, if there are imbalances in resources or resource consumption and where process tuning is required. This is strategic model validation.

Obviously, the BPM software must support the modeling of enterprise business processes before validation can be performed. The support for this in BPM software varies dramatically in style and scope. It is extremely important to assess BPM software against the needs of the organization rather than in a more general context.

Validation hinges primarily on simulation capabilities. The more complex and distributed the organization is the more important simulation becomes.

It is often the case (in both Strategic Process Modeling and Strategic Model Validation) that a BPM product specific to these functions will be used, although many BPM vendors are now including these functions in their products.

The key? Evaluate these functions against the needs of your organization.

Twelve

Human Interactions: No Cheese is Made of Chalk

By Keith Harrison-Broninski

(Adapted from *Human Interactions: The Heart and Soul of Business Process Management,* Meghan-Kiffer Press, 2005.)

INTRODUCTION: *In this chapter, Keith Harrison-Broninski, CTO of Rolemodellers Ltd., presents human interaction as one of the important considerations in the evolution of business and as a further example of how the impact and application of business process management extends to all of the critical dimensions where opportunity awaits us for the creation of business improvement and competitive advantage.*

There is common consensus that a modern business, if it wishes to stay competitive, must put in place efficient systems for management of its processes. It seems to go almost without saying that the solution lies in computer systems for Business Process Management. After all, re-arrange the words slightly, and the problem becomes the solution. If you need to sand a floor, you buy a floor sander. If you need to paper a wall, you buy wallpaper. If you need to manage business processes, you buy a Business Process Management system. And, for an appropriate price, there will always be skilled people willing to do the work itself.

But is it always so simple? What if you need to build a reseller network in Asia? Improve in-house design skills? Control the flow of commercially sensitive information outside the company? There are processes involved, certainly. However, it would take a particularly hard-nosed Business Process Management vendor to stand up and say to a board of directors that its software caters in itself to such problems. Existing process languages, for all their power, do not in themselves capture the human issues crucial to such activities. Why is this? And what else do you need?

Vendors of advanced process support software rightly claim that their products expose processes in order to render them more manageable. However, we will show that the processes typically exposed by such systems are of a specific type: centered on software applications. Hence, the benefit of expressing such processes via such systems is largely that you can then make better use of the software applications concerned—to re-use legacy applications, for example, or provide more sophisticated automation that joins up diverse applications. Is this the best we can hope for from process management? To answer this, we must deal with the underlying question—are all business processes about software applications? Are business processes just about executing transactions and keeping records?

Unlike cats, not all processes are grey in the dark. Every business person knows that not all the activity in the enterprise takes place within a computer. There are two major types of business processes, and these require different forms of treatment, both by managers and by computer systems. Unlike the mechanistic processes conventionally handled by process support systems, many business processes are essentially human phenomena—driven by people rather than by machines. There is a major new source of competitive advantage out there, just waiting for a new type of process management software—the Human Interaction Management System.

What is a process made of?

No cheese is made of chalk.
Three Voices, Lewis Carroll.

If we are to understand what current process modeling techniques can do, and what they can't do, we need to understand what they *are*. In particular, we cannot fairly judge the utility of these techniques unless we have a true understanding of what those who employ them mean when they talk about "processes"—since this may not be the same as we take them to mean. What are the nuts and bolts from which such a process is actually made?

Look at the Web site of a typical process support vendor and you will see a range of product descriptions, ranging from prophetic claims of step-changes in IT thinking, through to sturdy reassurances of scalability and robustness. You will get support for massive parallelism, transparent messaging both within and across organizations, automatic handling of failure conditions, Old Uncle Tom Cobley[1] and all. But what is being run in parallel? What messages are being sent? Failures in what, exactly, are being handled so well?

It is necessary to pull back the wizard's curtain, and look at the fundamental components of the typical business processes implemented by current enterprise systems. This is possible since all mainstream process languages, standards and protocols share the same basic constructs. We can see this by looking at a graphical notation recently devised for diagramming processes, the Business Process Modeling Notation (BPMN)[2]. This notation sets out specifically to be a way of depicting business processes that is *universal*—applicable to any business process whatsoever. BPMN lets a process modeler specify that:

- Specific things happen at specific times (Event triggers);

- A sequence of activities should be automated (Control flow);

- A big process is made out of smaller ones (Composition); and

- More than one thing can happen at the same time (Parallelism).

This is certainly useful, but nothing new. A process represented by BPMN can be coded directly using any modern, low-level programming language—Java, for instance, for which there is now a huge range of mature and effective tools and methodologies. So why use a process support system at all?

The benefits of defining processes as separate entities have been promoted by business theorists for a long time now, but until recently, technology did not permit end-to-end implementation of processes on an enterprise scale. A common perception of Business Process Management is as workflow "grown up"—*enhanced* to cater for fuller automation (perhaps by incorporating Enterprise Application Integration tools) and *extended* across (and between) organizations.[3] Some software vendors go even further than this, and claim that their systems operate fundamentally at a *business* level. These vendors assert that their systems can be configured to get work done simply by "calling down" into lower-level components of the technology stack and, ultimately, application programs—thus obscuring low-level technology details from the business user entirely.

In other words, the IT department is not intended to remain in control of how the technology stack is used, but to pass control over to the business. Moreover, process support systems, once built, are supposed to be easy to change—because they are expressed at such a high-level, essentially that of the business itself, and you can map business changes directly onto new process definitions. Well, perhaps. And perhaps not yet.

Typical process support systems, in their current incarnation, are unlikely to fulfill this vision, since the underlying process languages from which they are constructed aren't designed for such purposes. Consider BPEL,[4] for instance, a process language with the support of several major incumbent IT vendors, and therefore a likely candidate for future standard. Languages such as BPEL were designed to help technicians build automated process execution engines, capable of orchestrating distributed computing resources of various kinds—such languages were not intended to supply the semantics needed by a business analyst to carry out high-level process work. In fact, current work on BPEL is focused on driving down further into the technology stack rather than up into the business, with the creation of a low-level add-on that programmers can use to do even more detailed technical work.[5] For now at least, the high-level business-oriented process tier is having to wait, while the process world focuses on empowering IT developers to build business processes via programming techniques. For now at least, the users of standard process languages are not business people, they are not even business analysts—they are IT developers.

In fact, we see the same principle at work with another hot topic in IT, *Web services*. Much is made of the way in which advanced process support systems can call (or preferably, "orchestrate") Web services to create business processes. What *is* a Web service? It's a piece of function, generally implemented in some low-level programming language, and made available via the Web. Here again, low-level programs are the building blocks of supposedly high-level business processes. This has all sorts of implications, of which, two in particular jump out as having direct impact on the business. First, not many business analysts want to write computer programs, so the programmers are back in the picture. Second, once you have low-level programs as part of your process system, the sort of freewheeling on-the-fly responsiveness to business needs promised by process support vendors is just not going to happen—it's back to the IT department with a change request if you want something to work differently, with the usual consequent haggling over the delivery schedule.

Hence, most of today's process implementations are not, in fact, contained neatly in their own top tiers of the enterprise architecture, providing a simple translation from business needs to process implementations. Rather, the current Business Process Management *stack* is scattered across different levels of infrastructure as its designers require. Moreover, any serious process support implementation needs to make use of a range of other enterprise technologies—enterprise application integration, secure messaging, directory services, data management, and all the rest. It thus becomes part of a complex technology backbone, dependent on a range of other systems. Process support systems, as proffered by some IT vendors, are, in fact, new management techniques that help technicians handle the technology stack.

So, does this detract from the value of current process support systems? Not at all. Features such as *process projection*—linking individual functions in legacy systems together to create new processes—have enormous potential for cost-saving. Process projection provides the enterprise with the ability to migrate more easily to new versions of old systems, or to new systems entirely. Process projection also offers the chance to make the best possible use of existing applications by transitioning away from the processes that were originally hard-coded within them, toward a more adaptive framework that exposes processes and allows them to be changed as necessary.

Moreover, while enterprise systems have always been constructed from a range of technologies, we have always needed consistent interfaces, and standard technologies for federating and managing enterprise technologies. As the Business Process Management industry matures, it is driving the adoption of such interfaces and standards.

However, appreciating that a typical process support system is part of a more general technical framework does have deeper implications. Suppose one accepts that, as shown above, a typical business process implementation is essentially a new, higher-level approach to automation—essentially, a different way of creating and changing *programs*. Then some light is shed on the original question: What do most process support vendors, and most business process analysts, mean when they talk about "processes?" We can now see that the usual meaning of "process" is something very specific: *a sequence of activities driven by, and mostly carried out by, machines.*

In the book that spearheaded the Business Process Management movement, Smith and Fingar define a business process as: "the complete and dynamically coordinated set of collaborative and transactional activities that deliver value to customers."[6]

What we have shown is that current process modeling techniques and tools are geared toward activities that are transactional. So, what about the activities that are collaborative?

Straight away both the benefits and limitations of current approaches to process support are made clear. They let us *automate* as much of our business operations as we care to, and *routinize* other aspects via traditional workflow techniques. However, they do not deal with things that cannot be so easily automated or routinized—the dynamic, innovative, *collaborative* processes driven by humans. We know, however, that such activities exist. After all, if you are reading this, your job is concerned with them. But what characterizes them?

Human-driven processes

Processes don't do work, people do.
The People Are the Company, John Seely Brown and Estee Solomon Gray.[7]

We have seen how the underpinnings of current process implementations are essentially the same as the underpinnings of any modern computer program. A process suitable for expression in a process support system is assumed to concern *mechanistic transactions.* The basic principle is that you can understand processes by understanding the tasks carried out, the data operated on, and how they interrelate. This may be true for some business behavior, but surely is not true for all.

The mechanistic modeling approach works very well for certain processes. Many of the current Business Process Management success stories are drawn from areas such as manufacturing replenishment, factory control, financial transaction management, and logistics. Here the aim is to reduce human involvement to the minimum—not only to cut costs, but also to free up workers so as to allow more productive use of their knowledge and skills. As described above, the significant advances being made by process support vendors are to enable more complete automation of routine work and transactional activities.

However, there are other types of process in which human involvement should not, and perhaps cannot, be automated away. We might best describe these as *human-driven processes*. Consider, for example, complex sales, marketing, product design, negotiation, project management, and process design itself. Not only is it unfeasible to exclude humans from these activities; they are indeed the lynchpins of commercial success or failure. If you're good at such processes, you're probably good at business.

So, don't such processes deserve effective computer support, a Human Interaction Management System? For one thing, you cannot improve something unless you are able to measure it—so measurement tools for processes of the *human kind* should be of great value. In addition, even if automation is not the most important thing in these cases, computerized aid might still be of great value. Just to take a single example, *sales* is a critical activity in any business. Yet many salespeople feel they are poorly supported by the Customer Relationship Management (CRM) systems provided for their use.[8]

The underlying problem with systems such as CRM is that their aim is simply to provide information believed to be of value to those carrying out the processes concerned. There is no attempt to *manage* the processes. Hence, such a system offers no visibility of bottlenecks, communication failures, dependencies, goals, competencies, or any of the other aspects that an executive responsible for the process is concerned with.

This shortcoming seems a drastic one, given the importance of the processes. What can be the reason for this gap in process support technology?

Modeling the why and how

The red plague rid you for learning me your language.
The Tempest, Shakespeare.

The problem of computer support for human-driven processes may simply be that business analysts lack terms suitable for describing them. There are many management techniques based on understanding human behavior, ranging from human resources methods[9] through to project management theories.[10] However, not only is there a bewildering variety of such approaches, but no one approach sets out to provide a generic way of describing human-driven *processes*.

Hence, if you are responsible for a process such as complex sales, marketing, product design, negotiation, project management, or process design, you must find your own way to define and manage it. If you want business support tools, you must devise them too, either from scratch or by purchasing a package that has some in-built assumptions about how the process works. This situation is exactly what first work-flow, and then Business Process Management, set out to change.

However, most current process implementations don't cater to such processes. As described above, process support systems have generally been used only for the support of processes that could be characterized as *machine-driven*—sequences of tasks, sequenced and constrained via techniques drawn from programming languages. So, when business analysts come to analyze a business in terms of process, as often as not, human-driven processes are simply left out of the picture. Even on the occasions when an attempt is made to understand these processes, it is unlikely to succeed, because the terms available to describe such activities leave out so much of their essential nature.

Moreover, it is not possible to use conventional process modeling techniques to implement collaborative human-driven processes. In order to support human activity, a computer system must in some basic sense *mirror it*—provide a free-wheeling world of independent entities that know about each other, understand key aspects of the world with which they interact, are capable of communicating to each other this knowledge and understanding, and support any conceivable change on-the-fly. Such aspects of human activity cannot be captured via techniques designed primarily to specify the execution of tasks in predefined, if-then-else sequences, where the choice of what to do and when is made in advance by the process designer. To build support for human-driven processes, you need to use tools that make fewer assumptions about the world. In the words of Lewis Carroll, "no cheese is made of chalk." The stuff in current process modeling frameworks is simply not the same stuff found in human interactions.

So, what *is* the essential nature of a human-driven process? In machine-driven processes, it is useful to focus on *what* happens. By contrast, in human-driven processes, it is as important, if not more so, to look at *why* people do things, and *how* they carry them out. This is because, when people do knowledge work, the observed sequence of actions is just a corollary of why and how the actions are carried out. Unless you model the why and how, you will fail to understand the way in which processes can be carried out differently on different occasions. People tend to repeat, interleave and loop actions in ways that are not at all amenable to traditional analysis in "programmatic" terms.

Managing people as if they were machines is like trying to teach small children table manners. As soon as you've finished designing a process, the users will try to deviate from the expected behavior—usually when you least expect it, and with results that only create more work for their managers.

A step in the right direction is to think about actions as caused by business rules, rather than simply as a result of what has gone before.[11] Business rules are much more akin to the way people think about their everyday work than the programmatic "control flow" inherent in most process modeling techniques. In general, interaction workers do things *if and when* they need doing. They don't carry out fixed sequences of activities in the same order every day.

However, this provides only a small part of the answer. There are a number of other base concepts necessary to model human-driven processes.

In particular, it is important to understand the *Roles* assigned to process participants. The Role notion is absolutely fundamental to human behavior. We all play multiple Roles in everyday life, and adjust our behavior accordingly. A single job title generally conceals a number of different Roles—typically such different responsibilities as line management, client account management, financial reporting, operational activities, product direction, project management, and so on may be taken on by the same person at different times. These Roles need to be separated out if the underlying processes are to be understood.

Moreover, it is also vital to distinguish between a *Role* and its *User*—the person, organization or machine assigned to it. The choice of Users to play the Roles in a process has a fundamental impact on how that process will be carried out. Roles and Users are both important, and have quite different—although sometimes parallel—characteristics. For example, they both have *capabilities* and *authority*, but the terms do not refer to the same thing for a Role as they do for a User. The interrelationship between Role and User is critical to understanding how to manage human-driven processes. However carefully designed the Roles are in a process, it is likely to flounder unless the users playing those Roles are appropriately chosen.

To provide an overview of some of the fundamental concepts in human-driven processes, here is a list of example issues as they relate to a Role and to a User. This is illustrated by reference to *Complex Sales*, a process involving multiple vendor Roles such as Account Manager, Technical Support, Marketing, Sales Director, and so on (for simplicity, we leave out client-side Roles).

Role:

- *Goals* (the Account Manager tries to make his or her personal target).

- *Responsibilities* (the Technical Support must answer questions correctly and in a timely fashion).

- *Interests* (the Sales Director wishes to keep track of key sales).

- *Agreements* (between vendor and client there exist contracts, specifications, informal understandings, etc).

- *Private information resources* (the Account Manager maintains varied information about the client).

- *References to other Roles* (the Sales Director knows who his or her Account Managers are, each Account Manager knows how to get hold of the Marketing department if required).

- *Capabilities* in terms of actions that can be carried out (only certain Account Managers can grant high levels of discount).

- *Process authority* (Marketing has the final say on what promotional literature can be distributed).

User:

- *Identity* (a Sales Director will not entrust a key account to just anybody—they need to know that an appropriate person is taking on the Role).

- *Physical location* (the time zone of the user assigned to Technical Support may be important if phone calls in office hours are required).

- *Virtual location* (if it is necessary to get hold at short notice of the Sales Director, his or her mobile number and email address must be known).

- *Relationships* with others (it would not be sensible to assign to a client an Account Manager who is known to get on badly with someone in his or her organization; conversely it is wise to build upon existing working relationships where possible).

- *Behavioral tendencies* (a client whose preference is for extended and repeated meetings preparatory to purchase should be assigned an Account Manager with the necessary patience).

- *Capabilities* in terms of knowledge and experience (the user assigned to Technical Support should have the necessary skills).

- *Organizational authority* (a major client may feel slighted unless his or her Account Manager has a senior position in the vendor's organization).

The concepts above, as they apply to a *Role* (process participant) or *User* (the person, machine, or organization that drives a Role), find no place in conventional Business Process Management systems. Yet they are fundamental to the proper support of human-driven processes.

Having said this, some of the above concepts are catered for by existing modeling techniques based on role-based analysis of processes,[12] for which there now exist corresponding process enactment software and even a Business Process Management methodology.[13] However, in order to provide full support for human-driven processes, a process modeling technique alone is not enough. It is also necessary to understand *what sort of things go on* in a human-driven process.

Small talk

Human language can be used to inform or mislead, to clarify one's own thoughts or to display one's cleverness, or simply for play.
Language and Mind, Noam Chomsky, 1968.

We have seen that a fundamental aspect of human-driven processes is *collaboration*—human interactions, in which people co-operate to achieve individual and shared goals. So, if we seek to understand human-driven processes, we must ask, "What sort of things go on within a collaborative activity?"

A pointer in the right direction can be found in the theory of *speech acts.*[14] This is a way of describing human interactions that classifies them into a fixed set of types. There turn out to be a surprisingly small number of types that recur often in business. Most interactions can be classified as *request/promise, offer/acceptance,* or *report/acknowledgement.* Combinations of such "speech acts" can be built up to make "conversations" that capture much of what goes on in a business activity. A negotiation, for example, can be expressed as a conversation comprising a number of speech acts.

This approach, in itself, offers a useful device for analysis and support of human-driven processes, and software tools to support speech acts have been around for a long time. However, speech acts on their own cannot be used to model human-driven processes, or support them fully with software:

- First, there is no place in speech act theory for the aspects of Role and User discussed above. Without these concepts, each conversation effectively happens in limbo, without providing any of the information or insight that might allow management for improvement.

- Second, conversations cannot be defined in advance, then set into play like mechanical automata. Much of what happens in a human-driven process is concerned with deciding what to do next—in other words, the conversation is made up as it goes along. You might start with a basic notion of how the story will play out, but this doesn't last long.

For instance, suppose a specific team of designers is tasked to create a new type of switch for use in a car dashboard. Almost as soon as they get going, everything changes. The switch is actually made of multiple parts—so they split the team to work on each part separately, with the intention of integrating the parts at the end. Then some necessary expertise turns out to be missing, so new designers need to be brought in. They discover that some sub-components can be bought in rather then designed, although minor customization is necessary, so dealings with suppliers get complex. Just as integration is completed, there turns out to be a safety issue that affects other components. On rectifying this, someone notices that there is a fault in a component of the switch itself. And so on.

This situation is not a special case, but the norm. All human-driven processes have this character. Once you set a human-driven process in motion, it generates one sibling- or sub-process after another. These child processes then do the same. And all the processes pass information back and forth among themselves. In speech act terms, they ask for things, deliver things, and bring things to each others attention. However, speech acts on their own do not provide enough information to make sense of this—for you need to understand the *things* that are being requested, delivered and reported.

Returning to the dashboard switch, the designers will end up creating a number of drawings for different parts of the switch, interfaces between sub-components, interfaces between the switch and the rest of the dashboard, etc. They will also maintain fault logs, benchmarks, cost analyses, and so on. There are complex inter-relationships between these objects—so changes to some objects inevitably affect others. It is no good designing a sub-component that does not match the interface expected of it. Unless you can track dependencies, and understand the impact of changes, across a complex web of process information, you cannot manage the process at all.

So you need to know not only what sorts of conversations are taking place, but understand *what they are about*. In other words, you must understand the information that the process uses and creates, and the relationships between different pieces of this information. But if the process itself is a moving target, how can we possibly get a handle on the information that it generates?

To answer this question, we need to get away from current enterprise computing approaches to data management, and look at the way we humans really work, day to day.

All information is personal

Today's conventional operating systems force you to give every document a name, which is a nuisance and a waste of time.
The Aesthetics of Computing, David Gelernter, 1998.

Modern enterprise systems, in general, are founded on the separation of control flow from data. This follows from a general assumption, now standard in enterprise IT, that any and all business data should "live" in a centralized corporate repository, such as a database, data warehouse, file server, document/content management system or directory. Storing data in this way allows retrieval, maintenance and analysis tools to conceal the data's actual location from the business user, which makes it much easier for IT staff to maintain that data and keep it consistent. From the point of view of computerized process support, a process activity can make use of any such repository by invoking a tool to access it. In theory, this is a fundamental enabler, since it makes it possible to define processes without having to manage the data they operate upon.

That's the theory. In practice, only certain types of information are really centralized in this manner. Human-driven processes typically involve collaboration, innovation, discussion, negotiation—and such activities tend to result in a large number of document versions, notes, text messages, emails, letters, and telephone calls. All these are forms of information, highly relevant to the business, and potentially an important audit trail—yet no one would claim that all these are faithfully filed away in the appropriate corporate repository, grouped according to the process of which they form a part.

How could they be? There is an instinctive understanding that, in such human-driven activities, information is *personal*. Each participant builds up his or her own store of knowledge, and shares parts of this, now and then, with the others involved. Only in this way can the process move forward, since the nature of a human process is that we meet, go off and do different things, meet, go off and do different things, meet, ... and so on. The "different things" that we do when apart create information personal to each participant.

Could one insist that all participants start to keep everything they create—from a jotted down note to a text message to a revised document draft—in a single central repository? For a start, this would run the risk of imposing a stifling and unnatural block on progress, since the effort to file and maintain the varied pieces of information thus created would be an overhead no one wants. Moreover, even if you tried to enforce such a discipline, and accepted the consequent overhead, process participants may well be unwilling to work with it. This is for all sorts of reasons, not just the sheer amount of extra work that would be created and perceived as unnecessary by process participants. The most important reasons are to do with basic human nature. In such processes, we do not always wish to openly share everything we do the whole time. There are considerations of politics, courtesy, confidentiality, intellectual property, and just "readiness"—when you are first developing an idea, of any kind, it is natural to keep early versions private, or show them only in a certain form, only to a few chosen people.

You have to allow for this personal aspect of data both in your description of human-driven processes, and in the corresponding computer support. Otherwise, all that will happen is that people will bypass the system and do things the old way. It is an old adage of the IT industry that the success of any software is dependent on whether people "buy into" it. If a new system makes things that people need to do harder rather than easier, at best, they will pay it lip service; at worst, they will ignore it. Either way, the system will wither on the vine and never deliver on its promise.

So, suppose one accepts that personalized data is a feature of human-driven processes. A host of other considerations then come into play. Where is the audit trail of a process? How are document versions managed? What should be done about dependencies between different pieces of information? How can the enterprise know which document should be used for which purpose? What should happen when a document is discovered to contain errors or gives rise to problems? And, most importantly of all, how can process participants work together, if they each have their own, different data stores?

These problems seem very hard. Yet we cannot ignore them. After all, the same issues are there now, every day, as people work in precisely the way described above. These very real process problems are just brushed under the carpet, because at present there is no general attempt to manage such processes in a consistent or computer-assisted way. If we want to move forward, and look for what could be huge competitive advantage in dealing better with human-driven processes, it is necessary to grasp the bull by the horns.

What we need is some way to untangle the web of data—a simple approach to process definition that allows us to make sense of how personalized information is treated within the process as a whole. How can we sort the mess out?

Knowing what you know

To my surprise, it was my wife, I took down to Lamorna
Lamorna, English folk song.

We can get part of the way there by looking back at one of the notions central to human-driven processes: Role. In a human-driven process, personalized information can be handled simply by attaching it to a Role. Copies can be passed from one Role to another—and the original deleted if no longer required by the sender. Each Role can keep all versions of a particular document that it possesses, or just certain versions.

This gives us a way of storing information that is more appropriate to human-driven processes than using enterprise repositories. However, it does *not* give us a way to tell which documents are to be used for what. Returning to the dashboard switch, "Which designs should we base the final product on? What do we need to change if a particular supplier goes out of business? What actions should we take if a fault becomes apparent?"

Perhaps we need a "document relationship management" system to track all this. Hold on though—we must be careful not to fall again into the CRM trap. Document relationship management can provide us with vital facilities such as audit trails—which are a *legal* requirement in some areas. In safety engineering, for example, a crash investigation may require production of all written material, down to notes in a log book, as evidence in a court of law. This "product assurance" requirement is so stringent that engineering companies commonly resort to handling it by deleting any extraneous data, which only hinders problem identification and resolution.

This drastic approach to dealing with the problem is forced on the engineering industry, since just keeping copies of everything is not enough on its own—it doesn't tell you enough about what was used where, how, and for what reason. Unless document management is intimately tied into the *processes* that create and use the documents, it will be an expensive waste of time. For example, the answers to all the questions above about the dashboard switch depend on what exactly is going on in the switch design process, and those related to it—what version(s) of the switch is (are) in production, what arrangements we have in place with suppliers, who is using the switch and for what.

So, in order to manage our documents, we need to know "what is going on" in the process—"where we are," if you like. What deliverables have been accepted, problems identified, resolution strategies put in place, information requested, services contracted to customers—it is these *agreements* that determine the relationship between documents.

It's not *document* relationship management that we need—it's *interaction* relationship management. If we are to manage human-driven processes, we need to get a handle on the information generated by these processes, which means tracking, at a detailed level, what happens in the interactions between the Roles that own this information. What benefits will accrue from this?

Getting on better with each other

The only source of war is politics—the intercourse of governments and peoples.
On War, Clausewitz, 1832.

In principle, people seek to work well together, and managers seek to enable this. In practice, however, working well together is hard to achieve. Even in the best human interactions, there is often a lot of wasted time and effort, as people have to repeat requests for the same information, end up in meetings to which they have nothing to contribute, wonder whether or not they have made themselves clear, and so on. People may try to take this kind of thing, annoying as it can be, with a good grace—but things more detrimental to the business can be the norm. In the worst (but common) case, people don't understand the actions of others; they can only feel they are being treated unfairly; they start responding poorly to other process participants—and you get a vicious circle that is hard to break.

If we are to genuinely improve human-driven processes—and deliver competitive advantage from the activities of the workers who carry them out—it is necessary to put in place an environment in which each participant is able to *understand the actions of the others*. This means understanding the *interactions* in the process—for, by definition, these are the only points of contact between participants. Hence, interactions are the only time at which one participant can gain knowledge about the others.

Focusing on interactions and their content, rather than on tasks (as in conventional process analysis) or on data (as in CRM), instantly suggests all sort of ways in which human relations can be improved:

- *Cultural clashes can be minimized, as can clashes of personality.* Both these manifest themselves in a variety of ways ranging from the order in which actions are carried out, to the way in which documents are written, to "token" gestures that may carry great significance.

- *Incentivization can be re-engineered.* In many organizations, it is only sales staff and their managers who are given additional compensation on an ongoing basis in accordance with the results of their work. This can lead to resentment among other staff, (for example, the technical support team who were the critical enabler of a sale), but even if no one minds, how much better would all concerned perform if they too were compensated fairly? Taking a process view of human relations even permits the fair allocation of reward to third parties such as suppliers, if that is desired.

- *Meetings can be streamlined.* Whether a meeting is a physical get-together or an electronic (audio, video or Web) conference, all too often many of those involved are not really required, at least not all of the time. Or the meeting accomplishes less than intended because someone who is not there should be. And who hasn't attended a meeting that had no clearly defined aim? Better meeting planning can only be achieved via better understanding of the interactions represented by each meeting.

- *Communication within a team can be improved.* In many collaborative efforts, a number of those involved feel they should be privy to information that others alone possess. Sometimes this is inevitable, but often it is just an oversight, because there is no way to see "who knows what." Feeling that you are out of the loop is disempowering, and can cause not only discontent but also resentment. Moreover, a very common cause of problems is that someone wasn't informed of something they needed to know.

- And so on.

Any good manager sees it as his or her duty to resolve these sorts of issues. But without an interaction management system that caters for Roles, Users, and the information that each of them owns, achieving this is at best a black art, and unlikely to happen.

Managing human interactions

You better start swimming
Or you'll sink like a stone
For the times they are a-changin'
The Times They Are A-Changin', Bob Dylan, 1963.

So, what is the *nature* of Human Interaction Management? In order to answer this, let's summarize the fundamental features of human-driven processes that require support from computer systems:

- *Connection visibility.* Collaborative technology must provide a strong representation of *process participants,* the *roles* they play and the *private information resources* that belong to each of them.

- *Structured messaging.* In the future, our interactions may still take place via email, the Web, or any other standard protocol, but if we are to manage them better, they must be structured for us, under process control, by software.

- *Support for mental work.* Human-driven process support must act to recognize the value of the information processing done in people's heads, and offer ways to manage and recompense it like any other form of activity.

- *Supportive rather than prescriptive activity management.* People take action in different ways on different days. One should not seek to change human nature, but to make the best of it by supporting such behavior patterns.
- *Processes change processes.* Actions and interactions in human-driven processes must be able to effect *continual change to the process itself.*

In order to provide systems to support these features, we need a corresponding theory of processes, one that forms a complete modeling framework for human-driven processes that is Role-based—it enhances and extends the existing notation known as Role Activity Diagrams, both to change some basic principles appropriately and to combine these principles with concepts drawn from social systems theory, organizational theory, cognitive theory, computer science and mathematics. We draw together key lines of thinking, old and new, theoretical and practical, to synthesize *social computing* with *mainstream information technology.*

Providing computer assistance for human interactions has many and varied benefits—not least that it brings along a new concept of *process management* that caters naturally for the monitoring of, and control over, the most persistent problem of the business world—*process change.* The theory of human-driven processes allows complex problems to be made simpler, responsibilities to be assigned where they belong, and process support to be given a formal underpinning that allows an analyst not just to define and implement a process, but also to *reason about it.*

In a world where government regulations, such as the Sarbanes-Oxley Act, are putting corporate transparency at the top of the board-level priority list, businesses are grappling with the need to support change on a daily basis. Businesses require a formal underpinning for process support that deals head on with continuous change, and provides guarantees that systems will perform as expected. Such reassurance is not just a nice-to-have; in today's business world it's a sine qua non.

Robust, scalable, certified Human Interaction Management software already exists, and more such systems will follow in due course. These systems are required to complement existing transaction-oriented process implementations, if we are to deal with the full range of processes that exist in every business.

The techniques and tools via which business processes are currently implemented embody a sequenced activity approach to computation that's not designed to support the free-wheeling interactions of humans. Consider what industry veteran, Paul Harmon, wrote about the main contender for a standard process language, BPEL:

> "Most people assume that a BPM system should be able to manage a business process that includes employee activities, as well as wholly automated activities. The current version of BPEL can only manage automated activities! Thus, although BPEL can function as an EAI component in a BPM Suite, it cannot function as the primary BPM engine. In other words, no BPM Suite, today, can rely on BPEL as its primary language. This completely undermines the possibility of using BPEL as a way of passing process descriptions from one tool to another, or of passing a company's process description to its business partners."[15]

A process language such as BPEL cannot of itself support human-driven processes—it has different uses, for which it is well-adapted. In order to cater for human-driven processes, the *collaborative* as opposed to *transactional* face of business, similarly well-adapted tools and techniques are required.

This new category of enterprise system—the Human Interaction Management System—is a player that will sit alongside transactional process support systems to complete the business process picture. Human Interaction Management will *overarch* enterprise technologies to support human-driven processes, just as conventional process support tools and techniques *underarch* enterprise technologies to support machine-driven processes. The two approaches to process support will cooperate naturally with each other and with all other forms of enterprise software to realize the vision of the process management pioneers—to make processes the foundation of the enterprise IT architecture.

The Human Interaction Management System has emerged in response to the need for control over human-driven processes. It is the missing link in enterprise IT required to fill the gap left by today's transaction-oriented systems—and the early adopters will be the ones to reap the most competitive advantage.

Putting it all together

We are seeing the transformation of corporations into "real-time enterprises" that place as much emphasis on providing great product services as on making great products. A real-time enterprise accomplishes its work and innovates via a dynamic supply network (rather than a static supply chain) with lightning-fast response to ever-changing customer needs. In this new world, companies are competing on their processes. So, let us suppose that *human-driven* processes are truly the next step in process management, thus driving competitive advantage. What then will lead a company to industry domination?

Human-driven processes can only be understood—and hence managed—via the interactions between their Roles, and the Users that drive them. To do this, you need to manage:

- Both Roles and their Users,

- The information within the Roles,

- How this information is used in the tasks and conversations that constitute human-driven processes, and

- How each human-driven process evolves as it is carried out.

In the real-time age, the process-managed enterprise will dominate by implementing radically new means of support for human interactions. Winning companies will deploy innovative information technology tools to manage Roles and Users, capture information deeply personal to Roles, and help process participants use this information both individually and *collaboratively*. A new breed of software, the Human Interaction Management System, will provide the freedom that interaction workers need so that they are helped, and not hindered, by *the system*. With Human Interaction Management, smart companies will be able to optimize the human-driven processes that are, in the end, their people's jobs—and the next source of competitive advantage.

Human Interaction Management permits suppliers to establish a fundamental integration with the needs of their customers, by engaging directly with the human-centered processes for which their products will be used. In the twenty-first century, where customers are bewildered by choice and seek *understanding* from a supplier as well as low price and efficient delivery, such integration may be a necessity. Customers will find a supplier that they trust, engage with them, and stick with them. Anyone can compete in this heady new world—but to keep the customers you gain, you need Human Interaction Management.

Now is the time for companies determined to dominate their industries in the decade ahead to embrace the future of process support.

References.

---

[1] The English folk song *Widecombe Fair* is about a horse, borrowed by people who don't understand her capabilities, and who thoughtlessly overload her with "Bill Brewer, Jan Stewer, Peter Gurney, Peter Davy, Dan'l Whiddon, Harry Hawke, Old Uncle Tom Cobley and all." Eventually the poor horse just keels over and gives up, returning to haunt the moors as a ghost.

[2] Business Process Modeling Notation (BPMN)—see
http://www.bpmn.org/Documents/BPMN V1-0 May 3 2004.pdf

[3] While Business Process Management has its heritage in workflow there are two key differences:

1. Workflow focused mainly on document based processes where people performed the process steps. Business Process Management manages processes that encompass steps performed by both people and systems.

2. Workflow automated processes that existed with an individual department. Business Process Management addresses processes that can span the enterprise. Business Process Management technology must therefore provide far higher degrees of scalability than workflow.
(http://www.staffware.com/software/process_management/bpmfaqs.jsp?m=c6 #5)

[4] OASIS Web Services Business Process Execution Language (WSBPEL), commonly known as BPEL
(http://www.oasis-open.org/committees/documents.php?wg_abbrev=wsbpel)

[5] BPEL is geared toward programming in the large, which supports the logic of business processes. These business processes are self-contained applications that use Web services as activities that implement business functions. BPEL does not try to be a general-purpose programming language. Instead, it is assumed that BPEL will be combined with other languages which are used to implement business functions (programming in the small). BPELJ enables Java and BPEL to

cooperate by allowing sections of Java code, called Java snippets, to be included in BPEL process definitions. (http://www-106.ibm.com/developerworks/webservices/library/ws-bpelj/)

[6] Smith, H., Fingar, P., 2003, "Business Process Management: The Third Wave," Meghan-Kiffer Press

[7] http://www.fastcompany.com/online/01/people.html

[8] To make a CRM system effective you must rely on, say, the sales executive doggedly entering data about product, opportunity, target industry and so on for each prospect. And they have to re-enter this information time and time again. No sales staff are tempted by the idea of spending a day on the road then another two hours entering what happened that day into the CRM system. Reward systems are another hazard. Seddon suggests that it will always be difficult to make sales people use CRM systems because "they are incentivised individually. So they don 't want to put their information in the public domain." In this climate, sales people will even falsify data to hide what they re up to. Many CRM installations are designed to monitor the sales staff as much as the customers. Not a happy situation for either the system or the people using it. (http://www.themanufacturer.com/content_detail.html?contents_id=2732&t= manufacturer&header=reports)

[9] such as Belbin team roles (http://www.belbin.info/)

[10] for example, Coplien's organizational patterns (http://users.rcn.com/jcoplien/)

[11] This is known as *state-based workflow*.

[12] in particular, Role Activity Diagramming (RAD)

[13] Riva (http://www.mkpress.com/OULDdesc.html)

[14] See, for example, "Using a Language Action Framework to Extend Organizational Process Modeling" (http://www.cems.uwe.ac.uk/~sjgreen/UKAIS2003.pdf), which shows how speech acts can be layered on top of Role Activity Diagrams to provide a deeper understanding of interaction dynamics.

[15] Harmon, P., 2005, "BPEL and BPM," http://www.bptrends.com/deliver_file.cfm?fileType=publication&fileName=bp temailadvisor012505%2Epdf

Thirteen

Applying BPM in Manufacturing

By Michael McClellan

INTRODUCTION: *In this chapter, Michael McClellan, CEO of Collaboration Synergies, Inc., delves deeply into the role of business process management in manufacturing to uncover the value of BPM to this critical market segment while presenting the clear message of how BPM principles can best be applied to produce real value and sustainable competitive advantage in any industry.*

This chapter argues the use of BPM as *the* central tool to support next-generation business processes to transform the operations of manufacturers. Next-generation business processes? Dr. Max More, a strategic business futurist, postulates the process-driven enterprise, in the foreword to the book, *The Real-Time Enterprise*,[1] "The ideal vision of the process-driven RTE is one of companies where information moves without hindrance, and business processes are continuously monitored and trigger rapid reactions, usually automated according to embedded business rules. RTEs also sense shifts in tastes and practices and respond by offering new products and services. Automated processes easily traverse corporate boundaries, time zones, media and systems. Batch processes and manual input are minimized by ensuring that real-time information among employees, customers, partners and suppliers is current and coherent. The Now Economy is the instantaneous, frictionless economy of economists' legend—the mythical beast that may finally be emerging from the mist. The Now Economy is a web of RTEs that form a virtual supply and demand chain continually seeking information, monitoring, and responding, guided by humans, mostly at the highest strategic level." A flight of fantasy? I think not, for Dr. More's vision is indeed possible by harnessing the universal connectivity of the Internet with the emerging category of business software, the business process management system.

But why should companies bother taking the journey to next-generation business process management? The notorious Willie Sutton provided a crystal-clear answer when he explained why he robbed banks, "because that is where the money is." In manufacturing companies, there is a great opportunity for business process management because that is where the money is, and will be, well into the future. Massive assets (plants and inventories), extensive value chains, highly fragmented information systems, global resource availability, and the necessity to build and maintain competitive advantage are driving companies to innovate with their core business process, and collaborate with those processes across the value chain. It's the entire *value delivery system* that creates distinctive value to the end customer, not just a single company in the value chain. Business process management provides the tool set that can most effectively manage the end-to-end, multi-company value chain.

Today, most manufacturing companies have Enterprise Resource Planning (ERP) systems firmly in place, and Customer Requirements Management (CRM), Product Lifecycle Management (PLM), and Supply Chain Management (SCM) applications are on line. The general IT strategy has been based on implementing such enterprise systems to achieve best practices and cost efficiencies. However, with all the newest technology firmly in place, there are some operational capabilities missing:

- Major information system applications are still merely *islands of information*, leaving obvious gaps that prevent holistic, end-to-end process interactions between participants that drive the overall value chain.

- The promise of collaboration between entities (departments or companies) seems impossible due to wide systems disparity and the high cost of programming required to provide the desired integration of systems.

- Functional information exchange and interoperability, as seen from the managerial perspective, is still frustratingly lacking. Multiple departments within companies, and multiple companies in an overall value chain are still interacting by "throwing stuff over the wall" to each other.

Such fractured information systems point to the need to reassess a company's information systems structure if they are to address fundamental changes in how to respond to increasing market pressures. The key change considered here is the ability to manufacture to actual demand, not to a forecast or master schedule—*make-to-demand* vs. *make-to-forecast*. There are many terms in use that describe this concept including lean manufacturing, demand-driven manufacturing, sense and respond manufacturing, and so on. All are based on the same idea of setting internal and supplier manufacturing requirements based on demand signals, not on forecasts or master schedules. After all, by definition, forecasts are wrong. Implementing business processes that support demand-driven objectives requires capabilities to *act* on information being generated throughout the value chain in order to respond in real time to individual customers. In other words, even having instant information available via the Net is insufficient, for it's the ability to act on that information that counts—and that's where BPM comes in. It's a huge shift from just listening-to-demand to making-to-demand.

Taking advantage of business opportunities in a real-time environment has long been the Holy Grail of business, but real help may be on the way if we explore how businesses can operate with a process-centric view, instead of following functional or departmental routines. The process-centric view begins with examining end-to-end business processes that cross all entities that make up the complete value delivery system. Unique restraints within manufacturing have prevented taking such views in the past. Manufacturing companies across most of today's value chains have small, individualized, standalone systems that have been installed over the past 20 or more years, as depicted in Figure 1.

Applications including programmable logic controllers (PLC) have been applied in a piecemeal, departmental or functional basis, with little or no thought given to the broader picture of enterprise-wide processes. Whereas accounting and other financially-oriented software has developed to a level of consistent broad-vision best practices—primarily enabled by enterprise resource planning (ERP) systems—engineering, manufacturing, logistics, and supply chain applications have not risen much above a functional view. The reasons behind this are many, but the essential restraint is the physical uniqueness of manufacturing facilities and processes (big investments) that limit how things are done, which, in turn, define the application of supporting information technology.

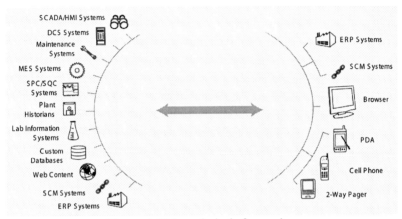

Figure 1 Value-chain information sources

Although manufacturing software applications have contributed substantially to modern manufacturing practices, they have been applied to fit the historical confines of existing processes within highly-specialized, functional departments. The result is a hodgepodge of very effective localized applications, quite disconnected from the higher-level business processes of the overall enterprise. And, as general systems theory teaches, it's the performance of the overall system, not just its parts, that counts. In a typical plant there can be as many as 40 disconnected and disparate plant systems. In a complete value chain, this number of information systems can rise to hundreds, each carrying out specific business sub-processes, without achieving the *overall coordination* vital to building a true competitive advantage—it's the end-to-end value delivery system that must be optimized, not just the individual parts.

This splintered approach to plant applications is changing as companies take advantage of newer collaboration, information sharing, reporting, and process management opportunities that are being applied in many forms.

Product Lifecycle Management (PLM) provides the ability to share information and collaborate on product design with value-chain partners (customers and suppliers). PLM has emerged as a significant management tool, especially in industries using outside contract manufacturing facilities, and those with multiple engineering and design locations. Included in this category is real-time information sharing for product tracking and product genealogy throughout the life of the product. This information can include the complete product design history from initial concept to product disposal, quality assurance data, engineering change order history, and use and repair information throughout the useful life of the product to disposal or recycle. There are pieces of this PLM concept available today, as shown in Figure 2, but they are often standalone, monolithic systems. The adoption of BPM tools represents a breakthrough to *coordinate* individualized solutions for an entire supply chain, yielding what may best be called *process-oriented PLM*.

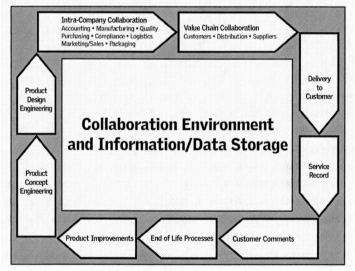

Figure 2 Product life-cycle management

Inventory and Production Synchronization is an approach to synchronizing inventories across value-chain partners. This means removing the inventory buffers that most companies put in place to protect their ability to provide products to customers when unanticipated events impact the production plan. Another major factor is basing production plans on demand forecasts and schedules that are shared between supply-chain partners as much as practical. Part of this trend is the growing requirement of mass customization to meet individual customer desires—Dell Computer's make-to-order model. Inventory management is a crucial element in accomplishing individualized unit production without a major adverse cost impact, and the goal of inventory management is to produce to *actual demand*, not anticipated or forecast demand. Using BPM tools to link together and coordinate the various sub-processes of participating suppliers that span the entire value delivery system is a monumental breakthrough that enables the make-to-demand scenario.

Distribution Order Fulfillment pressures have many companies implementing Collaborative Planning, Forecasting, and Replenishment (CPFR),® a model developed by the Voluntary Inter-industry Commerce Standards Association that is rapidly gaining importance in retail industries. This system of joint demand development has been implemented by a number of companies, building on earlier models of vendor-managed inventory (VMI), to improve capacity utilization and inventory management. Again, the challenge isn't just abut sharing demand information, it's about having the dynamic business processes that can respond to demand information.

Manufacturing Enterprise Collaboration recognizes that it simply makes good sense to share information. As our information technology applications have matured, we have developed large silos of information that have provided more and even better data. Unfortunately, we have constructed walls around and between function-specific business processes. These walls exist between departments within companies and between supply chain network partners in spite of the best efforts to date. The need to tear down information systems walls also becomes evident with the requirement to link companies and facilities that have come together through mergers and acquisitions. Although there might be a quick connection at the planning system level, the real-time process coordination, from the plant floor to the boardroom, is essential.

Historical efforts to tie manufacturing enterprise systems together through tight integration has been very expensive, unreliable, time consuming to develop, and difficult to change once in place. Collaborative manufacturing processes use disparate systems as network nodes that are linked to create higher-level processes in which all affected systems contribute sub-processes. One example is to link quality assurance processes from within the manufacturing execution system to a supply chain's event-management system, triggering relevant process execution in, let's say, planning and scheduling processes. To extend this further we might collaborate with downstream partners using the quality assurance processes, incorporating their scheduling and logistics processes.

Demand-Driven or Lean Manufacturing is a general approach to manufacturing to the current requirements of the customer. This is not based on annual master schedules with monthly releases. Instead, it's based on constantly fine tuning the relationships between entities of the value chain, driven by actual demand signals. Linked processes between Wal-Mart and their suppliers provide point-of-sale information within hours to give the value-chain participants a near real-time view of inventory and sales trends. Likewise with Dell's make-to-order model, customers configure their own products, and the demand signal travels straight through to Dell's suppliers' and contract manufacturers' processes—they are all one, a holistic value delivery system.

Regulatory compliance and Business Performance Management (that other BPM) are driving an entirely new set of reasons to better support business processes. Whether it is Sarbanes-Oxley, FDA CFR 11, or WEEE (Waste Electrical and Electronic Equipment), it is the metrics associated with the business processes that confirm compliance. In addition, there are a number of terms being used in manufacturing companies to describe the use of information systems to measure performance. These includes Key Performance Indicators (KPI)s, Business Activity Monitoring (BAM), Dashboards, and Business Intelligence. All are based on the fundamental idea of using information from the originating source, collating the information to fit a broader user format, and presenting the result in a business process context that is near real-time. It's not just the changes in data that are important as a business metric, it's also measuring the performance of processes—where are the bottlenecks, which processes failed, and so on? This is not about online reports showing what happened yesterday or last week. The idea here is to present contextual information on processes as they are executing, in time to respond optimally with decisions that are based on a uniform view of a long-lived process.

Process Collaboration is the simultaneous use of real-time information across the value chain, not just to share data in real time, but to *act* on that information with business processes. In a contributed chapter in the book, *The Death of E and the Birth of the Real New Economy*, Dr. S. P. Rana elaborates, "Collaboration—and, by association, 'collaborative commerce'—are popular terms today. But collaboration is certainly not a new concept. Most companies collaborate in some capacity today, and indeed have been doing so for some time (albeit not necessarily well). For example, manufacturing-oriented companies are often not good at selling, and 'outsource' the function to distributors (channel partners).

"According to Webster's, 'to collaborate' means 'to work together [to achieve a common goal], especially in an intellectual effort.' The goal in commerce, of course, is revenue and profit growth, which ultimately stems from customer satisfaction. But companies don't always view their products and services from the perspective of customers. If they did, they would see that their offerings are but singular components of a holistic solution, and would place much more emphasis on their collaboration capabilities.

"Collaboration technologies fall into one of two basic categories:

- unstructured collaboration, which includes document exchange and sharing, shared whiteboards, discussion forums and email (*aka information collaboration*); and

- structured collaboration, which involves shared participation in business processes (*aka process collaboration*)."

"Even though it's sometimes referred to as 'collaboration,' *process integration* should not be confused with *process collaboration*. *Process integration* involves connecting—in a send-respond fashion—well-defined 'internal' (ERP) business processes, which are typically transactional in nature. For example, Company A sends a purchase order to Company B (a function of Company A's purchasing process); Company B sends Company A a confirmation (a function of Company B's order management process). Whereas this type of interaction has been facilitated in the past by fax, email or electronic data interchange (EDI), the modern approach is to utilize the Internet for inter-enterprise process integration. This type of inter-enterprise integration—sometimes referred to as Business-to-Business integration (B2Bi)—is a natural outgrowth of enterprise application integration (EAI), the focus of which was on the intra-enterprise (i.e., 'inside the four walls')."

"*Process collaboration* involves two or more parties participating in an iterative, negotiated business process, that process being more relationship than transactional in nature (e.g., coop marketing vs. a purchase-sales transaction), to achieve a common goal. Indeed, the intended goal of the process is a key factor in determining who does what, and when; which in turn implies that a process collaboration system is adaptive to changing business conditions. *Process collaboration typically supports inter-enterprise business processes that heretofore have not been automated*, [emphasis mine] due to the inability (until recently) of technology to support the constant fluctuation of collaborative relationships."

To support this world of collaborative business processes,—*creating powerful inter-enterprise business processes where none existed before*—a new view of the value and use of plant and value chain information systems must be taken. Such "emergent," end-to-end processes that span the entire value delivery system are the secret sauce for competitive advantage in manufacturing. Manufacturing systems have long played the Rodney Dangerfield role—a role where they could not get any respect. Compared to ERP,CRM, SCM and other so-called enterprise systems, production support applications, such as manufacturing execution systems or warehouse management applications, were frequently treated as unwanted step children. Though needed, loved, and protected by departmental managers, most plant systems have been difficult to justify on the basis of reduced costs and usually fall below the radar of corporate information technology managers. But the times are changing. There is now much greater value being placed on the information detail that is generated and used by business processes within the production and logistics world. This is where the value-adding action is in a manufacturing company. As businesses move closer to operating in a near real-time environment, reports that are records of yesterday's events are simply too late, or do not have enough detail, to support everyday business decisions and trigger appropriate action. In the sense-decide- and-react environment of modern businesses, it is the metrics data generated as events are occurring that provide the best basis for management decisions and actions.

It is difficult to identify or define the full range of applications used to accomplish production because industries are different and vendors have never hesitated to add to the confusion with labeling to suggest differences. A useful definition of production systems begins with a holistic view that includes the complete production system infrastructure, that is, the entire collection of business processes that provide the management and execution of production requirements. Many of the typical plant processes are shown in Figure 3. Although the term has wide meanings, these applications can be described as the manufacturing execution system (MES) or the enterprise production system.

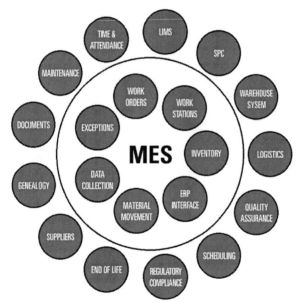

Figure 3 Manufacturing execution systems

Life would be easy if the plant processes were as simple and orderly as the illustration suggests. Unfortunately, reality is a bit messier, with plants typically running 20 to 40 different applications that have been installed over the past decades. Within a multi-plant company or within a supply chain, hundreds of disparate systems can be found. The value of these applications has typically been based on each system as a stand-alone answer to a particular set of operating conditions. The aggregate value of the manufacturing execution system is not considered, because business tends to think of these applications with a data-centric, functional management mind set.

The functional view is narrow and focuses on the requirements to support a specific manufacturing process, causing the functionality to be designed and built with a very inward sense. As an example, consider an application designed to support the quality assurance department. Although important quality management issues (such as statistical process control, non-conformance measurement and statistics, corrective action support, in-process tests, and more) are usually included, rarely will a software package address or have any connection to equally important issues such as WIP tracking, cost variance, or scheduling. Early material requirements planning (MRP) systems were often described as closed loop systems. The operator entered data, the software did the calculation, and clear truth emerged. It was indeed a closed loop that focused on internal mechanisms (pure logic unadulterated by outside forces) to deliver an answer.

This inward focus toward a narrowly identified list of departmental functions is what drives the frequent reference to many plant systems as *islands of information*, as depicted in Figure 4. Although ERP systems made a contribution to integrating islands of information, much greater value can be envisioned when we alter our thinking away from functional management to an enterprise-wide, process-centric mind set.

The value of the information changes when used to support higher-level, enterprise-wide business processes. For example, a given business process has one value when developed for a department supervisor, and quite another value when also used to meet Sarbanes/Oxley compliance needs. Another example is how the value of quality assurance information increases substantially when used to support enterprise-wide warranty exposure issues. Inventory management processes take on a different look when viewed across a value chain with synchronized schedules based on real-time demand. This greater value comes by changing from a functional view of manufacturing applications to a process-centric view where the higher impact, end-to-end company processes can be supported. After all, that's what customers see, the value delivery system in its totality.

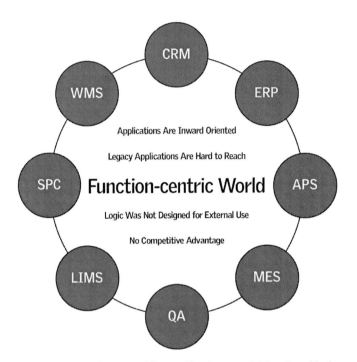

Figure 4 Function-specific applications and islands of information

The hard part about incorporating isolated production processes into wider use is the problem of exposing sub-processes into a context that supports an overall enterprise business process. Historically, this has been very difficult. Most information technology departments are not closely connected to plant operations or various MES components and have very little awareness of what processes are available or how to access them. A medium-sized facility could have sixty or more disparate components within their MES. Many of these applications were built to specifications long since forgotten using technology that is no longer current. Documentation is frequently poor or nonexistent. Further, when the desired processes have been identified and located, the cost and time to integrate the work processes on the plant floor have been prohibitive.

Vendors are improving process accessibility in different ways. Many are moving to broaden their product/function footprint. Most have perceived the necessity of including a wider range of information in their systems, often with a particular emphasis on quality assurance, product lifecycle, and genealogy processes. Other vendors are building extensive product offerings through acquisition, with the apparent plan to integrate this functionality into modular product suites. There are a few companies that are providing a fully integrated MES that includes modules for warehouse management, scheduling, product data management, process modules, maintenance and repair, quality management, and Web services. This is great for the future, but the real issue is what to do with our currently installed base, especially when you consider the disparate systems scattered across the many companies that make up a given value chain. How do we take this vast information resource from a function-specific, inward focus, to a higher-level business process support mechanism? We should start by examining what a process is.

A process is a *coordinated* series of steps or tasks aimed at accomplishing a defined business objective. There are manufacturing processes, accounting processes, credit approval processes, material receiving processes, inspection processes, product design processes, and so on. A business can have hundreds of processes and most processes can be broken into sub-processes and components that include people and information system resources. Ideally, processes within a company are related, and all aimed, directly or indirectly, at serving customers. In many industries it's not the product that differentiates one company from another, instead it's the processes used to meet customer requirements, as demonstrated by Dell Computers. It is this process-centric mind set that successful companies are using to keep and sharpen their competitive advantage.

Processes have generally developed around commonly accepted business practices. In many companies these practices and associated processes have never been questioned. Today, extensive operational improvements can be gained through simple observation of how existing processes work, and seeking improvement alternatives. Examination of how work gets done has come about due to modern business systems such as ERP that are based on and require consistent business processes. Optimistically, what these systems have delivered are, in fact, best practices. Unfortunately, we all know even the best systems are silos of information with obvious voids that require people to do mundane tasks to make the business perform. BPM is aimed at filling those voids between existing processes buried in information silos. A few examples of the BPM advantage include:

1. Add functionality to existing enterprise systems such as CRM, ERP, MES, and so on.

- Extend an existing application using BPM rather than install new software or reprogram the existing software.
- Design and add new processes as requirements change.

2. Link business systems to aggregate end-to-end value-chain processes.

- Build new processes between separate systems to provide a full view of, let's say, inventory management and logistics systems.
- Connect MES systems within a value chain to support where-to-build strategies with real-time information.
- Connect disparate business intelligence sources within the company and across the value chain to support Sarbanes-Oxley compliance.

3. Link a number of systems to provide and support new processes.

- Build a process to provide demand-driven scheduling processes across a complete value chain.
- Connect the manufacturing execution systems to the planning and scheduling systems.
- Develop a process that allows certain CRM users to view and exchange data with the warehouse management and the manufacturing scheduling systems.

4. Design, build, simulate, and finalize new stand alone business processes using data and sub-processes from any source.

5. Address the opportunities of demand-driven manufacturing initiatives with critical information availability from any source in the value chain. Signals from end users can be directly connected to production and planning environments to allow proactive and correct responses.

In most manufacturing companies these ideas would require a significant investment in time and money and, most likely, will not fully satisfy the requirements when the project is finished. Typical implementation usually follows these steps:

Step 1. The functional manager or operations committee is required to define the desired new process, outlining in detail what is to be changed. This requires an "as is" view along with a "to be" vision.

Step 2. When the operations committee has completed its homework the project is turned over to the IT department for development and implementation. IT is not typically sitting on its hands with nothing to do. IT staff have a backlog of work that requires the new project to be examined for its worth and put into the queue based on some evaluation process.

Step 3. The IT analyst begins by delving into the project requirements and examining the ability to satisfy the project needs using as many existing information tools and data sources as possible. A budget has been set and it is the analyst's job to meet the requirements within the cost constraints. Based on the analyst's concept, a detailed plan is built identifying all the systems work necessary to do the job. A fundamental part of this is the graphical outline of the process indicating process steps such as events, inputs, decision points, and so on.

Step 4. The programmers swing into action, developing new code to fit the application based on what they interpret from the analyst's presentation. Code is written and tested, and equipment is purchased.

Step 5. The finished product is presented to operations. Necessary changes are made to debug the system, respond to new requirements, and address requirements that could not be met.

Step 6. The operations committee finalizes and accepts the end product in spite of changes that should be made based on items not seen prior to coding and implementation. Business conditions have changed and some revisions to fully satisfy the users are requested. IT is busy so the requested changes must be again put into the queue awaiting action. Typically, when there is available staff to make the changes, the original person or group is on another project and the learning curve restarts from some point just above zero.

This cumbersome development process creates what has been

called *the great IT divide*—that no-mans-land between IT departments and the operational departments that rely on them. A significant promise of BPM is to radically alter this very difficult relationship by a) vastly shortening the process, perhaps all the way to zero code; b) putting the process more or fully in the hands of operations; and c) building and implementing processes in a way that they can be *easily* and *quickly* designed, developed, simulated, revised, implemented, and revised again and again as necessary to meet changing business needs.

BPM is a great advancement from hard-programmed workflow systems, but a company is still *not* going to turn process development over to the janitor. This is very serious work that requires understanding the current state of existing processes within the company, and being able to visualize the new. A key perspective here is to see BPM as an *enabler* of business process change, not as a gee-whiz technology for technologists. Where applications such as CRM, ERP or MES are assortments of technology functions, BPM is a tool that allows users to design, build, and implement business processes that suit their ever-changing needs. As Microsoft Word is a tool to create and manage documents, BPM is a tool to create and manage processes.

With BPM, process development is speeded up by process analysis components used to model the new process, identify the operations required, identify and locate the sub-processes and convert all this to a new or improved operating process. The process can be simulated to identify any operational problems or design faults. The process can be revised with each change identified and tracked, thus building a process lifecycle history. Other versions of the same process could be used to accomplish other tasks. The beauty of the BPM approach is the ease of process development and implementation. The ability to simulate the process and observe actual performance brings great real-time management control. Process changes do not require coding, but, instead, are accomplished through applying icons from a process-modeling palette. In fact, it is likely that a large number of processes will be developed and applied with copies held in libraries for later use in other requirements. Another approach is to use slightly varied instances of a process, such as order entry process, each designed to fit a specific customer or group of customers such as Wal-Mart, Sears, Safeway, Albertsons, and Target. It is likely that each target company has its specific process requirements that you, as a supplier to them, must meet.

Begin your process journey by assessing where you are and how BPM technology might affect your company over the next few years. Examine your ability to make changes to processes, or even understand how the existing processes work or were developed. Think in terms of end-to-end, cross-functional requirements that begin with the customer and conclude as a satisfying financial return—e.g., order-to-cash. If the vision is adequately holistic and seen from the highest level, lower-level processes and their intersection with departments and information sources will be somewhat self-evident.

BPM is rapidly gaining attention in manufacturing industries, with major analyst firms estimating growth as high as 30% or more per year. After some initial assessment, it would be surprising if you could not see major opportunities for improvement by using this tool, and most vendors are eager to accept a challenge to examine your needs and develop an initial demonstration and proof of concept that can be very inexpensive and frequently done in a matter of days. BPM is not a panacea but it is an excellent tool set that makes revision and enhancement of your existing information technology much easier to realign to meet ever-changing business process requirements in a fiercely competitive global economy, characterized by overcapacity. In Dr. More's Now economy, the manufacturer that dominates its industry will do so by making the right product, at the right price, at the right place—right now, for that's what today's customers demand.

References.

---

[1] Fingar, Peter and Joseph Bellini, *The Real-Time Enterprise: Competing on Time,* Meghan-Kiffer Press, 2004.

Fourteen

Five Fables and Their Lessons

By Martyn Ould
(adapted from *Business Process Management: A Rigorous Approach*,
Meghan-Kiffer Press, 2005)

INTRODUCTION: *In this chapter, Martyn Ould leads us through Five Fables in a provocative expose to uncover the true breadth and depth of this thing we call business process management. The perspectives presented in this chapter are sure to trigger some new insights in BPM, while bringing to light considerations of successful BPM that are often neglected.*

Do your toes curl when someone uses the phrase 'paradigm shift'? Did they curl just then? Terms like that get debased so quickly, we just as quickly learn to treat them as noise. So, when a real paradigm shift comes along, it needs a lot of volume to say 'THIS REALLY IS A BIG CHANGE, GUYS'. Business Process Management is one such.

The key thing about a paradigm shift is that old ways of thinking just won't work in the new world. If your structural engineers have only had mud to work with in the past, their ways of specifying and designing buildings will be fine for mud buildings but they won't make a lot of sense when the steel girder appears on the scene. In particular, you probably won't ever have had the idea of the staircase – just what is an 'upstairs'? If you live on a group of small islands in the ocean, you might never have needed the wheel and hence will never have developed a mechanical theory of gearing, but you might have developed some very sophisticated ways of thinking about the design of paddles and hulls.

Let's be clear. Until recently we've supported our organisations with *information* systems. Because computers started out as … computers, things that computed, early computer language development focussed on doing computations on numbers – what we call 'arithmetic'. FORTRAN was (and still is in some areas) the language for arithmetic computation. When useful amounts of storage became a realistic proposition and symbolic data could be kept *about* things, languages shifted slightly to the side and added ways of describing symbolic as well as numeric data and of 'computing' with data – typically moving it around and rearranging it. COBOL was (and still is in some areas) the language for handling arbitrary data, such as text. Even workflow management systems were, at heart, information processing systems with a veneer of process on top of a database: process *added* to data.

The traditional paradigm views organisations as things that work with information, so our systems have been about looking after information. In the past we have specified our information systems in terms of what data they will store and how we can access it and change it and move it around. And we have designed our information systems in terms of data representations and operations on data. Our techniques for specifying and designing systems have been based on data processing and, more recently, object processing. The object-oriented world is one in which the 'object' takes centre stage and our data is data about objects and our processing is driven by objects and their communications. The big paradigm shift of the 1980s was about replacing data by objects at centre stage. It took a lot of shouting then to get people to listen. And it needed a new raft of ways of specifying and designing systems to exploit the new paradigm: new languages, new architectures, new methods, new ways of thinking.

But now, with BPM, our systems are looking after *processes* – a bigger paradigm shift still. When processes take centre stage, how must we change our ways of thinking about the organisation? Neither data-based nor object-based styles of thinking are going to work for us – they underpin the old paradigms. (We're sure to see desperate attempts to use languages appropriate to data and data computation to describe the world of mobile processes: IDEF0 is one notorious example, and UML another. They won't work. If you've always built boats, a wheeled vehicle will be beyond you.) The process-oriented world needs process-oriented languages. The business process world needs business-process-oriented languages. Data-oriented and even object-oriented languages and methods can only be tortured into supporting business process thinking – they don't have the concepts necessary. Process-oriented languages need process-oriented methods – like *Riva* – to make them work for us.

In this chapter we'll explore some of the aspects of the new paradigm that will change the way we specify and design process management systems, as opposed to data management systems. In five fables and their consequent morals, we'll look at the new challenges that BPM forces us to address, and we'll characterise the solution. We'll be looking at things that we have not had to worry about in a data-oriented world.

Our first fable is about the apparently simple challenge of deciding what processes an organisation must have. Traditional methods pressed into use from the world of data processing only lead us down a dead end, and we need a new approach which a Tutor and Pupil will discuss.

The second fable challenges us to move from a world where data-based systems plumb individuals into their data to one in which process-based systems coordinate groups of collaborators. Data plumbing must be replaced by collaboration plumbing.

In the third fable, we address the challenge of getting our heads round the mass of activity that's going on at any one time. In the traditional paradigm, we worry about complexity in data; in the new paradigm we worry about concurrency of process.

Fable four moves the concept of 'process' centre-stage and brings home the fact that a process is not some static blueprint on the wall that we all glance at now and then: it has a life-time of its own: it is created, lives through change, and perhaps dies. Moreover, its growth and development don't just reflect or mirror or tag along behind growth and development in the organisation: they *are* that growth and development in the organisation.

The fifth and final fable looks at how our relationship with our systems must change too. Our current information systems are remarkably stupid, perhaps because they are *information* systems and know nothing about what we are doing. Why doesn't my PC 'know' I am writing a chapter for a book, and why do I have to name everything and remember where I put it? If our process support system just 'knew' what was going on …

Fable the first: Of axes and scalpels

Outside it was a clammy day. Dr Fostrup was relieved to get into the dissection room at the teaching hospital, swapping the humid, stale air outside for the faintly nauseating but cool air inside. Strictly speaking, it would not be he that would find the air nauseating, but the new group of medical students here for their first lecture at the dissection table. A few would pass out, but the paramedics would be there as always to carry away their limp bodies.

Boris could be relied on to have everything set up and ready: the cadaver, the dissection tools, the large screens for projecting close-ups, the thick marker pen. The full dissection would run over ten sessions as they got into ever more detail. A good start was essential.

A full house as usual, students sitting in steeply banked concentric circles around the table. This had once been a public spectacle but was now carried out with a little more decorum. Instead of beverages, the audience carried notebooks and pens, their purpose now learning rather than entertainment. The nervous murmur died away as Fostrup walked into the arena and approached the table. Pulling aside the cloth from the cadaver he wished the students 'good day'. Few replied.

He had never been one for too much chatter at the beginning and so, having donned the necessary protective clothing, he called for the axe. The paramedics stood by.

This was a heavy axe, quite difficult to control, but Fostrup brought it down swiftly and lopped off the lower part of the right leg. Boris stepped forward and wrote 'The A bit' in large letters on it with the marker pen. It was put aside on a nearby table. Five students were put aside on recovery tables outside. Those that were left dutifully recorded the name of that part of the body against their sketches of the body. Some were not quite sure where exactly on the leg the axe fell, but chose a point anyway, sketching a line somewhere around the knee area. A second blow separated most of the left arm from the body, and Boris penned 'The B bit' on it, again placing it to the side. Two more students dropped and were carried out. There was more scratching in notebooks.

Fostrup appeared to think for a moment but then quickly lopped off three more pieces which Boris labelled 'The C bit', 'The D bit, and

'The E bit'. The students continued to take notes, but were becoming increasingly unsure about exactly how much corpse each bit was made up of. Some glanced at their neighbour's drawing to double check that they had caught the correct point where a bit had been lopped off. The big overhead monitors helped but it seemed everyone had a slightly different view.

Boris labelled what was left on the table 'The F bit'. Everyone wrote 'The F bit'. Fostrup paused. Up till now he hadn't uttered a word except for 'good morning'. But he now confused everyone by starting to talk about some research in psychology that suggested that the brain could hold only seven, plus or minus two, ideas at any one moment. Indulging in a little obligatory irony, he noted that for students the figure was more probably five or six, and concluded by saying that it was for this reason that he would stop lopping pieces with the axe, now that there were six big pieces in all. 'The F bit' was still quite large however, so, asking Boris for something a little smaller, he took a substantial meat cleaver and deftly chopped the F bit into several pieces which Boris promptly labelled 'The F1 bit', 'The F2 bit', and so on. The students were getting rather frantic now as they desperately tried to gauge where the blade had fallen so that they could record those points on their sketches. As they strove to keep up, Fostrup reached for a smaller cleaver and made three swift cuts to the F2 bit, pushing them across to Boris who marked them 'The F2a bit', 'The F2b bit', and so on. An eighth student finally succumbed and was labelled 'The G7c bit' by an unsympathetic friend before the paramedics could carry her away.

'That's all for today, ladies and gentlemen,' announced Fostrup, removing his overgarments and leaving. Students scribbled furiously as Boris removed the labelled bits to the refrigerated store for further decomposition at the next lecture.

Moral: When we chunk organizational activity into processes we must have a sound basis for that chunking.

Tutor

What understanding do the students now have about the way the body is constructed and how it works? Has the chunking been guided by an understanding of what a human body is all about? Would each student have the same understanding of exactly what constituted each bit?

If Fostrup gave the same lecture next week, would the student's drawings be anything like those of this week's?

We'd prefer that Fostrup had taken a scalpel with him to the dissecting room, together with an understanding of what a human body is all about – the fact that there are 'natural cleavage lines' that separate the central nervous system, the gastro-intestinal system, the skeleton, the musculature – and of how those systems are connected. We look for these things because we know that a human body is 'in the business of' feeling and sensing, nourishing itself, standing and moving.

When we chunk all that organisational activity into separate processes, we shall need a similar scalpel that will allow us to cut along the natural cleavage lines of that activity, to separate out the processes using an understanding of what the organisation is all about, an understanding in particular of what business it is in. So how do we divide all the activity going on in the organisation into a set of processes in a way that is rigorously derived from an understanding of what business the organisation is in? These processes are what I might call *essential* processes because they are to do with the essence of the organisation and not the result of some design decision about how to do the business of the organisation. The other question I'd ask is whether we can do it in a way that yields the same answer whoever does the analysis and whenever they do it?

Pupil

I can't see why this is a problem. Surely we just need a chunking of some sort.

Tutor

If you and I walk into the same organisation's building together and go off, separately, and draw up a list of these essential processes that the organisation operates and their dynamic relationships – what I would call a *process architecture* for the organisation – what sense would it make if we came up with a different picture?

Pupil

But even if we drew the same picture, things will change tomorrow.

Tutor

I disagree. If the organisation decides to change how it's structured, why shouldn't the process architecture remain the same? Why should there be different essential processes if it's still in the same business?

Similarly, if the organisation decides to change its culture, why would the process architecture change? Why should there be different essential processes if it's still in the same business?

Clearly, how those processes are carried out will change if the allocation of responsibilities changes, or if the culture changes and the styles of interaction change with it, but the chunking will remain constant.

Pupil

I have this strange feeling that you're going to suggest that there is a process architecture for an organisation that is a sort of … invariant for it. Things are the way they are, the organisation has those processes, simply because it's in that particular business. Am I right?

Tutor

You're getting to know me. Yes, if we could characterise the business of the organisation in a way that is independent of *design decisions* such as the organogram and the culture and the technology it has deployed, then the 'chunking' of organisational activity into processes that we arrive at will be a firm rock on which to build all our other analyses of the organisation's business, for building BPMS-based systems for instance. Put simply, for an organisation in a given business there is a given process architecture.

Pupil

I'm sitting here trying to imagine what *would* change the process architecture of the organisation – I can see that a change of culture, or organisational structure, or of how the organisation wants to do its business wouldn't affect it, but presumably if the organisation changed *the business it was in* … that would change the process architecture?

Tutor

Precisely. I can put that another way: the process architecture is determined only by the business the organisation chooses to be in, and we can define that in terms of what I call essential business entities: things that represent the essence of the business the organisation is in. Let me just say for now that in the architecture we'll find two sorts of process: *case processes* and *case management processes*.

A case process is one that deals with one something, to be more precise a 'case' of one of those essential business entities. So we might have a process called *Handle a customer order*, or *Handle a clinical trial*. As you can imagine, at any moment there will be many 'copies' of each case process running, one for each customer order or clinical trial. I'm going to call those copies 'instances'.

A case management process is one that deals with the flow of cases: so we would have processes called *Manage the flow of customer orders*, and *Manage the flow of clinical trials*. As you might expect, given that it is all about scheduling, resourcing, prioritisation and so on, there is only one instance of each case management process at any time, overseeing the changing set of instances of the case process.

Pupil

OK, so when we walk into the building we know that there is a particular set of case processes and case management processes, and that we will have potentially many instances of the former and one instance each of the latter.

Tutor

Right, and all of these process instances are active concurrently and can be interacting. Case process instances obviously interact with their case management process instance – they report on progress, for instance. But process instances are interacting all over the place, and indeed causing new instances to be created. When I run a drug development programme (a case process) I need to get going a number of concurrent clinical trials (another case process), and once those clinical trials are operating I shall need to interact with them – to guide them, get their results and so on. Our process architecture will tell us the principal interactions that are there because of the business we're in. But more interactions will arise when we design the individual processes.

Pupil

Let's see if I have this right. What we actually observe in the building is a flux of interacting process instances, to use your jargon. And the process architecture would tell us what processes there are to be instantiated, when they are instantiated, and how instances subsequently interact?

Tutor
    Exactly. You know, you're really getting the hang of this 'instantiation' thing.

Fable the second: Of batons and conversations

– (slip stored at 12:54, fetched at 13:21) George, what do you make of the new communications system that's being proposed for next financial year?

– (slip stored at 13:22, fetched at 13:55) I think it's a brilliant idea, Lisa. It would be a great improvement on today's paper system.

– (slip stored at 13:55, fetched at 14:14) Yes, these 'teleferns' they're proposing to give us all would make a big difference.

– (slip stored at 14:17, fetched at 14:37) Well, you and I agree on that, but I was at a meeting yesterday where some of the Old Guard were still speaking up for the Paper Vault. Our consultants were there putting forward the advantages. They went through the whole thing. How the Paper Vault means a phenomenal number of paper Written Slips being carried from the sender to the Vault and then back out to the recipient. How we have to employ a mass of Couriers to carry them back and forth, not to mention all the Vault workers filing and fetching the slips.

– (slip stored at 14:41, fetched at 14:52) Too true Lisa, and *they* won't be pleased when they hear about it – most of them will be out of a job when the teleferns get installed and we can speak and record directly into this new Voice Vault instead. Electronic Speech Clips – a great advance. I still think there's something missing though … but I must get this off to the Vault for you.

    Moral: Collaboration is at the heart of real-world processes and must be at the heart of our process methods.

Pupil
    This is an example of what I believe is called 'paving cowpaths'?

Tutor

Indeed: 'We've always done it this way, so let's automate it.' In this case I think it's one step worse and they are in danger of paving a cow pat. Can you characterise the situation for me?

Pupil

Well, the people working in the organisation do seem to know about and engage in conversations: in this case George and Lisa are having a relatively informal interaction discussing a new technology leap ... though I'm not sure in which direction. The system that's in place seems to be built around storing word strings ... on these Written Slips. No notion of a person-to-person conversation: you seem to have to store and fetch slips that reside in this Vault. Bizarre. And now they're planning to pave that cowpath by allowing people to speak the slips into an electronic version of the Vault. But the old store'n'fetch paradigm is still right there, up front. I suspect that George is about to twig that if they could just recognise the idea of a 'conversation' between two parties and connect the teleferns end to end, person to person, instead of into the Vault, they just might make a real leap forward.

Tutor

Right. They'd move from supporting the individual with a store'n'fetch system to supporting collaborators with an interaction system. In a business process we *collaborate* ... act together, *inter*-act ... in a whole variety of ways:

We discuss something.

We negotiate.

I contract with you to do something.

I delegate a task to you.

I ask you for something.

I give you authority to do something.

We agree on an action.

We jointly approve something.

I instruct you.

You report your status to me.

I oversee something you are doing.

You pass me the results of your work.

You and I work on something together.

I chase the progress of your work.

So. when we come to think about and design real, collaborative business processes, we'd better have ways of doing it that have the concept of interaction between parties at their heart.

Pupil

Well, I've drawn flowcharts showing workflows.

Tutor

And do your workflow diagrams show who does what?

Pupil

Yes, if you add 'swim-lanes' and show the work moving from one person to another.

Tutor

What do these diagrams mean by a swim-lane? And what do they mean by a line that crosses from one swim-lane to another?

Pupil

I hadn't thought about it much. I guess a swim-lane represents a job title or perhaps a department. And a line represents where the activity moves from, say, one department to another. Sometimes we add the flow of stuff – data, materials, whatever.

Tutor

That's a very impoverished view of the world. I've got a picture of these swim-lanes as little islands with stuff moving from island to island. I can see boats travelling from one to another carrying batons that say 'your go now' and perhaps some stuff to go with the baton. Are organisations really just islands with batons and stuff moving between them? What are we doing here, now, for instance?

Pupil

Well, we're discussing the nature of processes.

Tutor

Right, we're having an interaction. We're doing something together. And in this case there's no stuff 'changing hands'. We aren't islands with boat traffic between. I'd hope that our process modelling approaches recognise that very important fact: when we interact – when we collaborate – we do things together. We don't simply send the boat over with a baton and some stuff on board. Quite the opposite: in business terms, interactions aren't just about the locus of activity moving from one role to another: real, business-oriented, value-adding things can happen in an interaction. Interactions are just as vital to the process as the actions that individual roles carry out on their own islands. Ineffective interactions can be as damaging to a process as ineffective actions. Slow interactions can affect cycle times as much as slow actions. So let's forget swim-lanes as islands and think about rich interactions.

Let's go back to the question of what the swim-lanes represent in the real world.

Pupil

Well, as I said, they're ... job titles, say.

Tutor

I'm bound to ask why you're starting with job titles. Let's stand back. When a process runs, *responsibilities* come and go. When a new customer order arrives, it creates a responsibility to deal with it. (In the jargon, the responsibility is instantiated, a new instance is created.) This in turn generates (/instantiates) further responsibilities that will contribute. The process is all about the coordination of all these contributions, all of these micro-responsibilities.

Pupil

I guess I can understand that: when we define someone's job or the job of a department, we effectively bundle up whole classes of responsibilities and say 'These are the ones you deal with ... in this job.'

Tutor

Right. And when the process runs, new instances of these responsibilities are created, get carried out by the nominated post or department, and disappear. The posts and departments in the organisation are pretty much static things, but the responsibilities are dynamic: they come and go.

I use the term 'role' when talking about those bundles. If we take a rather abstract view of the world, we can think of a role as simply a single responsibility that can be instantiated dynamically. If we take a rather concrete view of the world, a role might be a post on the organogram to which we have allocated a bundle of responsibilities.

Pupil

You're drawing a distinction here: our design of the process determines what responsibilities are created when, and how they interact; and our design of the organisation determines which roles are tasked with which classes of responsibilities. If we get that design right – if we get the collaboration right – things work. If not, not.

Tutor

Right. So, think of it this way. If we were to design a process in terms of pure responsibilities it would probably be quite simple. But then – for a variety of reasons – we design our organisation and carve up that neat process and hand pieces (i.e. classes of responsibilities) out to the posts and groups we have invented or which we find around us. Have you ever shared a pizza? All those strands of mozzarella between you and your friends – that's the result of cutting up that nice simple pizza and handing the bits around. And it's the same with processes. When we allocate responsibilities to different posts and groups we have to create interactions between them to make sure all those responsibilities remain coordinated, to make sure the right collaboration happens.

For me, a line between two roles is an *interaction*. That's an *inter-*action. And that's not the same as an arrow from one swim-lane to another. It's not that the locus of activity moves from one role to another – locus hocus pocus. It's that the two roles do something together: agree, decide, discuss, exchange, inform, request, report. These are more than data flows or control flows. The roles must interact in order to coordinate their responsibilities. Some responsibilities can only be carried out by collaborating with other roles. Once an interaction is over they can continue carrying out their separate activity until the next interaction. This isn't data flow. This isn't a flowchart. A line from one swim-lane to another is a poor thing, inadequate for capturing the interaction and coordination of responsibilities that actually takes place. Moreover, a swim-lane is a static thing, but in the real world responsibilities are generated dynamically.

In a sentence, getting our heads round the mozzarella (and not the other way round) means getting to grips with the responsibilities, their grouping into roles, their dynamics, and the interactions that coordinate their activity. With these concepts, we shall have a deep understanding of our process, rather than the skin-deep view we've become accustomed to – and all too easily satisfied with. Our process design method must give us the language to talk about collaboration and its dynamics.

Fable the third: Of bees, geese, and ants

– (CEO) Our consultants have drawn up process descriptions for our four main processes. I want the processes in place by the end of the month. This box contains a folder for each process. Let me know what you think by lunch time.

– (Minion) Yessir.

[Just before lunch time]

– (Minion) I've examined the folders. I found about thirty pages of text description for each of the processes. And a summary flowchart for each too.

– An excellent piece of work, don't you think? A good choice of consultants I made there.

– One question, sir. I took the smallest process – in terms of page count – and followed it through to get a feel for things. There's a very tidy flow from one end to the other.

– Yes, I insisted that they clean up the processes and made them easy to follow.

– Well, you could certainly put your finger at the beginning of the process and step through it till you got to the end, and in that sense it is tidy and clean. But if we were to implement it that way, and I were then to walk into the Analytical Department using the new process, I'd see only one person working at any one moment. Everyone else would be standing around waiting for their turn to come.

– I won't stand for that sort of inefficiency. Imagine an anthill in which the ants took it in turns. Or a bee-hive.

– Exactly sir. But that's what our consultants are proposing.

–Well, I want parallelism and lots of it, and I want it by the end of the month.

Moral: Text is serial but the world is massively parallel.

Tutor

Let's open a box on the process architecture – let's look inside a single process, one that could perhaps have multiple instances at any moment. What do we find?

Pupil

If I remember right from our last chat, we find a network of activity involving what you referred to as roles … each of which might be a single responsibility, or might be a bundle of responsibilities in the form of posts or departments?

Tutor

Right. And we said that these roles interact – they collaborate.

Pupil

Something tells me you're going to use the 'instantiation' word again.

Tutor

You're getting the hang of this. Of course I am. Responsibilities come and go: a customer places an order and a new responsibility is created to deal with it; you make a claim for expenses and a new responsibility is created to check and approve it, a responsibility that I as your line manager might be allocated to satisfy. So these responsibilities come and go – yes, they're instantiated. To generalise: such abstract roles are instantiated during the lifetime of a process.

Pupil

So we're not talking swim-lanes here?

Tutor

Absolutely not. The real world is dynamic. Swim-lanes are static. When a new instance of a case process is created to … let's say … carry out a clinical trial, a whole set of new responsibilities are generated related to that process instance: there's the responsibility for managing the trial, for developing the protocol for it, for recruiting patients for it, and so on. These responsibilities are created dynamically. Sure, they're handed out to people in specific posts or with certain job titles, but those posts and job titles are static things that could change tomorrow.

Summarise for me.

Pupil

Well, our process architecture ... our invariant process architecture for the organisation gives us a set of processes that can be instantiated, and as a result we see a constantly changing network of interacting process instances. And then within a single process instance we have a set of roles that can be instantiated and hence a constantly changing network of interacting roles.

Tutor

Yes, it's what we might call a *flux of concurrency*. But I want to add one more level: concurrency within a role instance.

Pupil

I almost suggested that. When I'm playing a part in a process there might be several things I could be getting on with: one bit of my brain might be dealing with getting the goods from the supplier and another bit could be sorting out the paperwork ... and I suspect there are more instances about to pop up?

Tutor

Right: you might be a programme manager ... a role that has been allocated a particular bundle of responsibilities ... and you might start collecting status data about all the separate projects in your programme. You email all your project managers at the same time, and then – in parallel – collect data from them, question them, and so on.

Pupil

So a role instance is itself a network of possibly interacting instances of threads of activity. I seem to have spaghetti in spaghetti in spaghetti ... to add to the mozzarella.

Tutor

Spot on. Concurrency is as rich a thing as collaboration. To really get our head round it at all three levels we have to capture the instantiation of processes, the instantiation of roles within process instances, and the instantiation of threads within role instances. Miss any one of these and we miss a chunk of the real world.

This ... terrifying ... flux of instances – of processes, of roles and of threads in roles – is what concurrency in the organisation is all about. And the networks of role instances and their interactions – within and across processes – is what collaboration is all about. If we don't have the right language and methods for dealing with this concurrency we shall either remain bewildered and hypnotised by it or fail to exploit it.

Let's think of our organisation (perhaps a hospital or a university) as a theatre. I'd like you to pursue the metaphor. Let's start with processes.

Pupil

Well, we've got processes – plays, I guess. Plays are written down in scripts ... process models, and ...

Tutor

Stop there for a moment. Think about performances ...

Pupil

Plays are performed ... they have performances ... process instances?

Tutor

Yes, keep going.

Pupil

So when we walk into the theatre we'll find performances of plays going on. Ah – the theatre seems to be a multiplex, because I have lots of plays being performed at the same time! Some plays are being performed many times simultaneously – those are the case processes. And some plays only have one continuous performance – those are the case management processes. Hmmm, worse still, some performances start up new performances! And presumably they have to find a stage to operate on.

Tutor

Concentrate on one performance for a moment.

Pupil

Well, a play involves of a number of roles. Each role in a performance ... ah, each role instance in a performance ... is acted by an actor – who was cast in that part somewhere along the line. Things start getting a bit weird around here, I suspect, because during the performance some actors might be acting several roles each, rushing around the stage from one to another. Worse, I suppose they might be acting roles in more than one performance, so they'll have to run from stage to stage, changing costume as they go. In the worst case they'll be acting several roles in several performances.

Tutor

When we're talking about an individual performance, remember we need to talk about role instances.

Pupil

Yes, that's a bit weird too: how many Hamlets can you have in one performance of *Hamlet?* Only one, I guess; but we certainly see processes in which some roles are instantiated many times – mercifully Shakespeare was content with a single instance of the Prince of Denmark on stage at any one moment. But it appears that in some plays new role instances are created while the play is in progress – as new responsibilities arise. And an actor has to be found to play each role instance. In extreme cases, the actors might be writing bits of play, inventing new roles, instantiating them, and then casting actors as they go along. This is truly contemporary!

Tutor

Absolutely. You mention casting …

Pupil

Yeeees. Presumably the allocation of actors to role instances is just more process … so casting happens on stage, and probably during the performance as the roles get instantiated – as the responsibilities get created!

Tutor

Right. Any thoughts about props?

Pupil

Well … the props are the resources an actor needs to play a role instance. It might be a book or a newspaper in a real play, and an information system or a software application in a real business process. Their costume sounds a bit like the mind-set they need for the role!

Tutor

So we have a number of stages, each with a performance of a play going on. Performances are starting up and stopping all over the place. On each stage, role instances are being played by actors, who are possibly rushing from play to play and from role instance to role instance, putting costumes on and taking costumes off, and picking up and putting down props as appropriate. So far so good. What about the actions that the role instances carry out and the interactions between them?

Pupil

I'm not sure I want to watch one of these plays. Sometimes a role instance is doing an action: so the actor is giving a soliloquy; sometimes it's interacting with another role instance – having a conversation – or even with several others at the same time. There may be several soliloquies and several conversations all going on at the same time in the one performance. And occasionally proceedings will get held up for want of an actor because they're acting another role instance on another stage. It's madness.

Tutor

Hold that thought. You've only dealt with role interactions in a single performance, but we know that process instances interact. And in the theatre?

Pupil

Oh dear. Some plays are connected. A performance of one play has to interact with a performance of another. That means that role instances in the two performances have to interact – there must be communications systems between the stages – telephones or email or something. Or perhaps the actors rush to and from each other's stage, or perhaps they meet in the corridor? My head is starting to spin.

Tutor

And well it might. But, when you get right down to it, this is exactly what happens in any organisation. A great flux of concurrent activity. We need process design and modelling methods that give us the concepts and language and grammar to get a handle on this.

Organisations achieve things from this flux. Nobody has their finger on a flowchart, tracing their way through until the goal is reached. There's no one thing in the process that is what achieves the goal. There no one thing under the hood of a Porsche that is its performance. That performance is an emergent property. When geese fly long distances, each bird uses the same tactic: fly in a specific relationship to the next bird. The result is a chevron of birds. That chevron is an emergent property resulting from the interactions and concurrent activity of all the birds. Yet no bird looks at the overall shape and decides how to respond. It follows its own tactic.

Likewise, the effect of the organisation is an emergent property resulting from the interactions and concurrent activity of many role instances across many process instances. Once again we see that if our process methods don't really get a handle on interactions and concurrency we won't achieve the emergent behaviour we are looking for.

Fable the fourth: Of lives and how they are lived

– Doctor, the system's asking for a name for the accident victim they've just brought in. Do we know it?

– No. Skip that screen.

– It won't let me.

– Put 'Donald Duck'. We'll fix it later if he survives to tell us.

– OK. It's asking for the treatment path we're expecting him to follow.

– Well, pick the appropriate one.

– There isn't an appropriate one.

– Isn't there an 'Other – please specify' option?

– No.

– Pick the nearest one that involves MRI scan and head X-rays. We'll work round it.

– OK ... but now it's asking for ...

– Where the hell did this system come from?

– General Admissions, I heard ...

Moral: Processes must have lives of their own and our 'language' for processes must allow processes to be the subject of processes.

Tutor

No-one would install a system so obviously unsuited to its purpose. But what's the problem?

Pupil

Well, clearly they've been given a system that assumes that the people it is supposed to be supporting use one process whereas in fact they use another. In fact, it's probably worse in that … I'm guessing here … medicine is very much about adapting the treatment process to the patient and to outcomes, and not to following one fixed process. And there's another dimension I could also guess at – one that has a longer timescale– namely that treatments change and technologies develop, and today's treatment process would need to evolve with those changes.

Tutor

Right. Moving a system with a fixed process from one department to another clearly makes no sense. It doesn't take much to see that. But your other points are good and I want summarise them by saying that *processes must have lives of their own* – they need to evolve. In fact we've just touched on three sorts of process evolution. Firstly, we would like to take a process from one place and use it elsewhere, but with adaptation. Secondly, we would like to be able to adjust a process to adapt it for a particular case. And thirdly, we would like a process to evolve as its environment (in the largest sense) also evolves.

Pupil

So the plays in the theatre aren't fixed?

Tutor

I'm afraid not. The scripts of plays can be rewritten. We might have liked *Hamlet* the way Shakespeare wrote it, but we might also consider changing it for modern times – strengthening the substance abuse angle at the end for instance.

Pupil

Eeeek. So who is it that is changing the script?

Tutor

That depends. In some situations the original author might come along and produce a new version, perhaps rewriting the final act to give it a different outcome, or refining some of the smaller parts for better characterisation, or removing unnecessary material. When a new performance of the play is about to start, the actors can use the new version.

Pupil

That's understandable in the real world: we have all sorts of reasons for wanting to change the way we do things – our processes. But presumably the whole business of changing a script happens outside the theatre?

Tutor

No! The scripts are in the theatre – that's the only place you can change them. Not only are they in the theatre, they are part of the subject matter of the theatre: in other words, you can get hold of them. Now, you can only change a script by using the *process* for changing scripts. *Handle a script* – let us say – would be just another process, indeed a case process, one with as many instances as there are processes/plays.

The whole point of this theatre is that it is where *everything* happens – there is no 'outside' – and one of the things that can happen there is that you work with your processes. Putting it another way: the theatre supports you *in* your processes, by managing all the collaboration and concurrency; but it also supports you *with* your processes, by giving you all the means you need to write new ones or change existing ones.

Pupil

I can accept that a script can get changed and new performances use the new script. But presumably any performance in progress is unaffected? Please?

Tutor

Why so? Why should a performance not switch to the new version as soon as it's available? Why should it be forced to carry on with the old one? In some situations sticking with an old script might make sense – for consistency reasons perhaps – but in principle we don't need to make performances stick with old scripts.

Pupil

I'm struggling … I have a picture of a 'master' script which could be changed. Any performance in progress might continue with the old version, or switch to the new version.

Tutor

Who said anything about 'masters'? Why shouldn't a performance use its own variation of a script?

Pupil

... because ... they ... OK, why not? So, they might start with the 'standard' script for Hamlet but decide to change it in some way for just this performance?

Tutor

Of course! They're doing a lunch-time slot, they're ten minutes in and realise that people don't have time for a full *Hamlet*, so they quickly do a rewrite and present a reduced version. There is nothing fixed or sacred about a process. Fitness for purpose, matching the process to the customer – those things are sacred.

Pupil

Now I'm getting concerned about the sort of chaos that will ensue if we let everyone tinker with processes as they please.

Tutor

Then don't let everyone tinker with processes as they please: you must script the *Handle a script* process to control what can and cannot happen to a script. Everything is in the theatre, including control over use of the theatre.

Pupil

My head is hurting.

Tutor

OK. Let's take a breath. Why don't you think through the implications of the existence of the *Handle a script* process.

Pupil

Well, I guess that for each script there is an instance of *Handle a script* running. Which means there is a stage where that performance is going on, and that performance has the actual ... the paper script on it. Presumably if someone wants to use the script they get it from that process, from that stage. They can take it away in some form and use it for a new performance on its own stage. So far so good?

Tutor

Yes. But I want to put what you said in a different way: *scripts can be handed around.*

Pupil

Oh dear. One performance can give a script to another performance?

Tutor

Of course. Processes are truly mobile. When an interaction occurs between two process instances, a process might be involved. In traditional computer systems, data was passed around, or messages were passed between objects. The object-oriented paradigm is only halfway to full process thinking: the unit of currency ought to be the process.

Pupil

One of the things that has really come home to me is that processes aren't – except in a few cases – simple static workflows. They evolve and blossom and die as the organisation 'runs'. And moreover they can be evolved and changed and developed as objects in their own right. I can see that instantiation is the key to this.

Tutor

Yes, and a good example is email. If you observe an email conversation – a process instance – you see it develop and spread and die back and stop. It can do this – in a way that a workflow cannot – because new participants can be brought in and introduced to each other, making new interactions possible: the process evolves.

Pupil

I'm beginning to feel that a workflow diagram with swim-lanes is only going to allow me to describe the simplest of processes.

Tutor

You're right. We need appropriate concepts, we need a language built on those concepts, and then we need a method using that language, that together give us a handle on collaboration, concurrency, and mobility. That way we'll get a valid and stable understanding of our business, before we set off trying to move our processes onto a BPMS.

(Meanwhile, backstage …

Oldie: You're new round here, aren't you?

Newbie: Yes. It's all a little scary.

Oldie: You'll get used to it. Things are very flexible. You'll fit in. They'll make sure of that.

Newbie: Who will?

Oldie Your owners.

Newbie: I thought I was … myself. No-one owns me … do they?

Oldie: Sure. In fact I can see someone who wants you approaching now. Must be off.

Owner: OK, you there, you're needed as you are on three new items and with variations on four more. Stages 12, 15, 523, 827, 828, 829, and 923. Move!

… while back in the classroom …)

Tutor

Well, we've pushed the theatrical metaphor a long way. But one thing that should have come out of it is that plays are not only being performed in our multiplex, they are also being written and adapted. Processes are the currency of the BPMS; but the BPMS is also the mint of processes. And of course we haven't said anything about information. There will be information 'in the system', but it will be attached to the performances – it will provide context for the performances, very much in the nature of props.

Pupil

Fine. But now I need to leave the multiplex for the city – I need to understand how this works in the real world! You pointed out that we probably won't allow uncontrolled change. But presumably this ability to change means that where once the imposition of an ERP required revolutionary change from the organisation, with a BPMS we can more easily accommodate evolutionary change?

Tutor

I'd take a more aggressive view and say that we can *exploit* evolutionary change, rather than just accommodating it, now that we have the methods for describing processes and changes to processes in a way that gets to grips with all that collaboration and concurrency.

Suppose we define a bit of a process for a bit of our department. What are the possibilities?

Pupil

I guess we could use that bit for a while and tune it, on-the-fly. Then when we're happy, we can grow the process to cover more of our activity or more of our department, or another department, or one of our suppliers or whatever.

Tutor

Yes. Now that we recognise a process life cycle – discovery, design, deployment, execution, monitoring, control, change – organisational change can be more continuous, more incremental, perhaps closer to the ideals of Total Quality Management, in that process-centric change is now in the hands of the actors – the process becomes the business of its actors.

Fable the fifth: Of names and the lure of names

...

– (Caller) But I rang at around 2pm yesterday.

– (Desk) I'm afraid I need a reference number to find the details of the case.

– I don't have a reference number – the case concerned is the one I called about yesterday at 2pm.

– I can't find things on the system if I only know when you last called about it. I need the reference number of the case.

– But you know who I am and I'm the one the case is about, why do you need to have some idiot reference number? The case I'm calling about is the same case as I called about yesterday – I'm simply picking up that conversation and continuing it. Why can't we simply carry on that conversation?

– I'm afraid our computer doesn't know about your conversation, it only keeps data against reference numbers.

Moral: When we design our processes, actors need only see their process context, not data names.

Pupil

Surely the Desk was in the right? When we store information in computers we ascribe it to the things we are dealing with? In this case the Caller was calling about some ... unspecified ... case and was simply being asked 'Which case are you talking about?' – and presumably the reference number would have identified the case concerned.

Tutor

Yes, but you've made two important suppositions. Firstly, you've supposed that a Business Process Management System is just another sort of information system. Secondly, you've assumed that we can be content to design systems from the point of view of the system and not from the point of view of the customer.

Let's take those two suppositions. Justify the second for me: that it's the system's point of view that is the important one.

Pupil:

Well, I obviously can't, especially when you put it like that.

Tutor

OK. The moral is that when the Caller called they were indeed simply carrying on a previous conversation. When they – as opposed to someone else – call, the system should (let me anthropomorphise for a moment) say 'Aha, it's Biggles calling – she must be carrying on that conversation we had yesterday. Where did we get to? I said I would get the details and tell her next time she called. What were those details? Here they are.' And then it should answer Biggles appropriately. Asking for a reference number is dumb.

I'll give you another example. When I sign on to my PC it just sits there and doesn't do anything. Doesn't it know what I'm doing? Clearly not. One of the things I want to do is work on this new chapter. In fact I am working on several projects right now, in different ways. I have to remember where in my folder structure I have put files about this chapter, and I have to remember what their names are: what did I call that file of typesetting instructions from the publisher for this book and where did I put it? Heavens, why am I worrying about the names of things?

Pupil

You just want things to do with that particular book on your desktop when you decide to work on that book.

Tutor

Exactly! We only give things names because we need to be able to find them again! I want the BPMS to know where I am with what I am doing, and when I ask to pick up the threads (of that role instance) I want to be presented with everything appropriate, everything in context. No more names! ... except for cases: I must be able to tell the system which book I want to work on ... which role instance I want to act ... but I don't expect to have to know where everything about that book is – it should just come to my desktop.

Pupil

If I can go back to where we started, I wonder if online shops are setting a small example: clicking 'Where's my stuff?' should show you a list of your stuff not just ask you for a reference number for your order.

Tutor

A nice example, even if it is something that can be done on a normal database system once you have identified yourself. But it does point up what is happening: if I might slip into my jargon for a moment, it's about connecting the actor to the role instance. Just as interactions are about connecting role instances. No more data engines – instead we shall have interaction engines. And our process design methods need to give us the means to think about processes in terms of interactions and to remove names.

Summary

These fables have highlighted some important aspects about business processes. We can summarise them in four words: *network*, *collaboration*, *evolution*, and *context*. These characterise the new paradigm, and they must be at the heart of how we think about our processes when we come to specify and design our Business Process Management Systems. Simply extending our information-based methods simply won't work – they don't have the necessary concepts at their heart. Let's recap.

When we watch the organisation, we see a flux of interacting process instances. Some process instances start other process instances. When their work is done, process instances die. Process instances interact. It's a dynamic network that changes as the flow of business through the organisation changes. We shall never understand how an organisation works by thinking in terms of some hierarchical chunking (remember the axe man?) – we can only understand it in terms of a network of process types that generates a dynamic network of process instances when it 'runs'.

And when we watch a process instance, we don't see a thread of activity running along: we see a flux of interacting responsibilities, each corresponding to an instance of a role type. Some role instances start other role instances. Some role instances die when their job is done, their responsibility accomplished. Role instances interact. Things get done because there is this network of coordinated activity, a flux of responsibilities collaborating to achieve a business goal. We shall never understand how a process works by thinking in terms of some hierarchical chunking of activity, or even a thread of activity flow – we can only understand it in terms of a network of role types (/responsibility types) that generates a network of role instances when the process runs.

The active organisation is a dynamic network of concurrent process instances, each of which is itself a dynamic network of concurrent role instances.

The process coordinates roles (/responsibilities) through their interactions: roles work together to get things done. By collaborating, the individuals generate the emergent behaviour required. Our processes are effective if that collaboration is smooth and smoothly supported. Our processes are efficient if we get the concurrency right and support it smoothly.

If we support a process with an information system, we shall be in danger of making the process the prisoner of the information system. Since we cannot contemplate revolutionary change simply to change our processes, we must base our supporting computer systems on our processes, and in a way that allows us to grow as we go, to adapt our processes to the changing environment. And this doesn't mean that we must have some sort of 'flexible' information system. It means that we must have process enactment systems in which the processes are themselves 'on the stage' where other processes are in place to allow them to be changed.

Finally, because people in the organisation (actors) are now process workers and not information users, our concern must be to connect each actor to the role instance(s) they are acting, and not to information according to access rights. That role instance will be associated with the information necessary to carry it out. The actor's context is determined by their role in the process and the state of that role, not by the information they have stored and now need to access.

The new paradigm of business process management needs new methods for thinking about collaborative processes and for specifying and designing business process management systems in ways that build on the concepts of *network, collaboration, evolution,* and *context.*

About the Authors

You can reach the authors by email:
authors@bpmg.org

STEVE TOWERS is the co-founder and CEO of the Business Process Management Group, a global business club (established in 1992) exchanging ideas and best practice in BPM and change management. The BPMG has now over 10,000 members across all continents and business sectors and leads the thinking in the BPM community. Steve is recognized internationally for his contribution to business process and change management, speaking and working throughout the world with leading organizations in the public and private sector. Steve is also one of the four co-developers of the 8 Omega Framework for Business Process. An innovative approach to BPM and change that enables organizations large and small to embrace BPM in a structured and inclusive way. He is an active practitioner working at the leading edge of BPM and understands the realities of implementing large-scale change in often complex environments. Steve's engagements cover all continents over the last decade with an easy and yet incisive style geared to helping people directly test the ideas, experience and solutions from the Business Process Management Group.

ROGER BURLTON is the founder of the Process Renewal Group. He is considered a global leader in the introduction of innovative methods for change and is recognized internationally for his pioneering contributions in Business Process Management since 1991 when he wrote his first papers, conducted his first BPM consulting and taught his first course. Roger has chaired several high profile conferences on BPM globally, including Knowledge and Process Management Europe, the annual National Business Process Re-engineering Conference in the US and Software World Canada. Roger also chaired the annual conference for the Business Process Management Group in 2003, 2004 and again in 2005 and has run the DCI BPM Conference series in the US for the past two years. His pragmatic BPM seminar series are the longest continuous series of their kind in the world. They run regularly in North America, Europe, Australia and South America and have been translated into multiple languages globally. Roger's highly acclaimed book 'Business Process Management: Profiting from Process' is regarded as the reference book for process professionals who want to actually conduct process architecture initiatives, and process renewal projects as well as those who wish to entrench process stewardship across the enterprise. Roger graduated with a B. A. Sc. in Industrial Engineering at the University of Toronto and is a certified Professional Engineer in the Province of Ontario. He can be reached at rburlton@processrenewal.com.

PETER FINGAR, Executive Partner in the digital strategy firm, the Greystone Group, is one of the industry's noted experts on business process management, and a practitioner with over thirty years of hands-on experience at the intersection of business and technology. Equally comfortable in the boardroom, the computer room or the classroom, Peter taught graduate and undergraduate computing studies in the U.S. and abroad. He has held management, technical and advisory positions with GTE Data Services, American Software and Computer Services, Saudi Aramco, EC Cubed, the Technical Resource Connection division of Perot Systems and IBM Global Services. In addition to numerous articles and professional papers, he is an author of the landmark books: *The Real-Time Enterprise: Competing on Time,* just-released, and *Business Process Management: The Third Wave,* now in its fifth printing *(www.mkpress.com).*

ANDREW SPANYI is the Managing Director of Spanyi International Inc., a consulting and training company in organization and business process design. He is the author of the book *Business Process Management is a Team Sport: Play It to Win! (www.mkpress.com).* His current practice focuses on assisting leaders to transform traditional mental models and behaviors towards ones based on enterprise business process principles. He was previously affiliated with The Rummler-Brache Group [RBG]. Since 1991, Andrew has worked on over 135 major performance improvement projects across several key industries in both the USA and Canada. Previously, he worked as a Senior Vice President at SCONA, a specialty financial services firm, and prior to that assignment he was the Director of Marketing and Product Development with Xerox Learning Systems (AKA as Learning International, Achieve Global). Andrew speaks regularly at conferences on Business Process Management. He has written extensively on business process issues and has had articles appearing in magazines such as Strategic Finance, Financial Executive magazine, Industrial Engineer, Manage Online, and on a number of Web sites including www.bpmg.org and www.bpminstitute.org. He holds a Bachelor of Arts (Economics), and earned his MBA from York University. He is an executive coach with the BPM Group, a Director of the Association for Business Process Management Professionals, and is affiliated with the Babson College Process Management Research Center. Andrew can be reached at andrew@spanyi.com.

ADRIAN GEORGE SAHLEAN, Principal at XCLSoft and Faculty Fellow at the Boston Graduate School of Psychoanalysis, is a published author who holds degrees in both Psychoanalysis and Philology. He brings his unique experience in counseling, coaching, and performance assessment to the understanding of how business process management is applied to corporate innovation and growth. He is the co-author to the upcoming book, *The Dynamically-Stable Enterprise: Engineered for Change (www.mkpress.com).*

VASILE BUCIUMAN-COMAN, Founder of eSkill, an online testing service, and of XCLSoft, a consulting company specialized in enterprise architecture. He holds a degree in Aeronautical Engineering and has more than 15 years experience in the IT industry. He held technical, consulting and management positions with companies like Spyglass, eSkill, Instrumentation Lab, Cigna, and PRTM. He is the co-author to the upcoming book *The Dynamically-Stable Enterprise: Engineered for Change (www.mkpress.com).*

MARK MCGREGOR Mark McGregor is a principal of the Business Process Management Group a global business club and is a recognized internationally for his contribution to business process, business modeling and enterprise architecture, speaking and working throughout the world with leading organizations in the public and private sector. Mark has worked with many of the worlds leading vendors of BPM solutions and is a well respected author and writer on the themes of business and process change. Mark is also one of the four co-developers of the 8 Omega Framework for Business Process. An innovative approach to BPM and change that enables organizations large and small to embrace BPM in a structured and inclusive way. Mark has recently contributed to publications such as CIO Magazine, Finance Today, and previously been published in Success Now, Enterprise Middleware, Application Development Magazine, Midrange Computing and Software Developer Magazine. He has also made contributions to two of the leading books on BPM, Peter Fingar's *The Real Time Enterprise* and Paul Harmon's *Business Process Management: A Managers Guide.* As a founding columnist for BP Trends Mark leads the thinking on the effective implementation of BPM Solutions and helps organizations bridge the divide between business and information systems.

DR. PEHONG CHEN, president, CEO, and chairman of the board of Broadvision, is an internationally recognized business visionary in the field of new media and self-service Web applications. He has received numerous accolades for his leadership at BroadVision, including Master of the Universe by Business Week as one of the 25 most influential people in e-business, Entrepreneur of the Year by Ernest & Young, and Fast500 by Deloitte & Touche. Prior to founding BroadVision in 1993, he was vice president of multimedia technology at Sybase, responsible for the company's interactive initiatives. Earlier, he founded and was president of Gain Technology, a leading supplier of multimedia software tools, where he pioneered multimedia as an enabling technology for a new generation of business applications. Gain was acquired by Sybase in 1992. He also helped found Siebel Systems, now a worldwide leader in front office automation software, and served on its board of directors until 1996. Dr. Chen received his PhD in Computer Science from University of California at Berkeley in 1988.

RONALD ROSS, recognized as the "father of business rules," is Co-founder and Principal of Business Rule Solutions *(BRSolutions.com)*. BRS provides workshops, consulting services, publications, and methodology supporting business analysis, business rules, and rule management. Mr. Ross also serves as Executive Editor of BRCommunity.com and its flagship on-line publication, Business Rules Journal, which also features John Zachman, Chris Date and Terry Halpin. He serves as Co-Chair of the annual Business Rule Forum Conference. He was a charter member of the Business Rules Group in the 1980s, and is also active in the OMG Business Rules SIG. Mr. Ross is the author of a half-dozen professional books, including *Principles of the Business Rule Approach,* Addison-Wesley (2003). Mr. Ross received his M.S. in information science from Illinois Institute of Technology, and his B.A. from Rice University.

DAVID LYNEHAM-BROWN is the Chairman & Chief Development Officer of the Business Process Management Group. David is a well respected coach and trainer and has worked with numerous Global 5000 firms across the United States, Europe, South Africa and Australia, including Lloyds TSB, Citibank, National Australia Bank, British Telecom, British Aerospace, Dupont and UK Civil Service. He has developed leading edge training and coaching in BPM, Business Analysis and Change Management and is responsible for the international accreditation status of the BPMG training programs. As a result of this work David has been invited to work with a number of leading international business schools, including Exeter Business School, to incorporate BPM training into their MBA programs. As a mentor and writer David is unique in his 'hands on' approach and accessible style which translates complex and technical topics into practical toolkits for organization thinking and practice. His writing has appeared internationally in the Institute of Management Journal, Project Manager Today, Pharmaceutical Times and Computer Weekly.

JORGE EDUARDO SOARES COELHO is a managing partner at SisConsult, a management consulting firm operating in Portugal since 1996. He is also an Assistant Professor of Management Information Systems at the University of Minho and at the University Portucalense.. Mr. Coelho is active in professional and educational organizations including serving as the Vice-president of the

Commission for Quality in ICTs (CS03) of the Portuguese Institute for Quality and President of the Consultants Academy of Portuguese Association for Quality. He has held numerous educational and management roles including: Lecturer at the Instituto Superior de Engenharia de Coimbra, Head of Department of the Regional Division for Management Control, Industrial and Administrative Organisation and Information Technology of the Portuguese Post Office, managerial responsibilities for the Information Systems and Technology Department at the Price Waterhouse office in Porto, and Lecturer in Management Information Systems at the European University in Portugal. He is the author of the *Learn Method*, a systemic and integrated, object-oriented BPM approach which has been applied by many companies. He is a regular speaker at graduate and postgraduate courses and seminars on BPM, Quality and IS strategy in most Portuguese universities.

TERRY SCHURTER is regarded as the leading independent BPM Analyst and heads up the Research and Delivery practice of the Business Process Management Group. Terry works with the leading BPM solutions providers to bring their tools and approaches to the attention of the BPM Community. He has written and authored many reviews, research pieces and original work appearing in CIO Magazine, BPM Today, and various in-house Fortune 500 publications. Terry is also one of the four co-developers of the 8 Omega Framework for Business Process. An innovative approach to BPM and change that enables organizations large and small to embrace BPM in a structured and inclusive way. Terry works at the leading edge of IT industry best practice in North America and Europe on the theme of business process change. He is well respected and highly regarded for his objective and insightful writings which frequently appear in many popular business journals.

KEITH HARRISON-BRONINSKI is author of the landmark book, *Human Interactions: The Heart and Soul of Business Process Management (www.mkpress.com)*. Keith obtained a BA Hons in Mathematics and MSc Computation from Oxford University. His first assignment in the IT industry was to create the central conceptual model for the UK government-sponsored IPSE2.5 project that pioneered the take-up of Role Activity Diagrams for process support in the late 1980's. He then spent many years as an independent IT and management consultant, working in a wide range of sectors, technologies and countries. Keith is the CTO of Role Modellers Ltd (rolemodellers.com), whose mission is to develop the ideas necessary to support human-driven processes, and implement software applications to support them. Keith designed the Human Interaction Management System, RADRunner, a dynamic process enactment engine based on Roles and interactions, and is currently working on a suite of visual tools for human-driven process modeling, monitoring, simulation, analysis, and archival. Keith is also the instigator of the Web forum Role Based Process Support, whose purpose is to discuss and synthesize work on human-driven processes (smartgroups.com/groups/roles). Forum members are drawn from varied academic and industry backgrounds, and debate approaches to social analysis of business processes. Membership is open to all and you are encouraged to join.

MICHAEL MCCLELLAN has over 30 years of experience serving and managing manufacturing enterprises. He has held a number of positions in general management, marketing, and engineering, including President and CEO for companies supplying capital equipment and material management systems to nearly every type of manufacturer. In 1985 he and a group of associates founded Integrated Production Systems, a company that pioneered the use of computer systems to manage and track production events on the plant floor. These systems are generally referred to as manufacturing execution systems and have found extensive use in varying forms in production facilities. His first book, *Applying Manufacturing Execution Systems*, defines manufacturing execution systems and explains the reasoning and history behind them. His newest book, *Collaborative Manufacturing: Using Real-time Information to Support the Supply Chain*, is the first definitive examination of collaborative manufacturing concepts. He is President of Collaboration Synergies Incorporated, an advisory company providing consulting services in the area of business process management, real-time manufacturing information systems, and collaborative manufacturing system development and implementation. He is a frequent speaker at companies and manufacturing conferences, has presented a number of papers on manufacturing information systems, and holds one patent. He can be reached at mm@cosyninc.com or www.cosyninc.com.

MARTYN OULD Martyn Ould is an independent consultant on the software development process and the design and diagnosis of organizational and business processes. A graduate of Cambridge University, he has over three decades of software development and business process management experience, working for leading software houses and management consultancies Deloitte, Praxis and Logica. He is a Fellow of the British Computer Society, a Chartered Engineer, and an experienced author. He regularly lectures to public, government and corporate audiences, and teaches at Oxford and Bristol Universities. Martyn has pioneered the development of the Riva method for business process management, and is author of the landmark book, *Business Process Management: A Rigorous Approach* (www.mkpres.com).

Other Books from Meghan-Kiffer Press

Business Process Management: The Third Wave
Howard Smith and Peter Fingar

The Real-Time Enterprise: Competing on Time
Peter Fingar and Joseph Bellini

Business Process Management: A Rigorous Approach
Martyn Ould, Co-published with the British Computer Society

IT Doesn't Matter—Business Processes Do
Howard Smith and Peter Fingar

Business Process Management: A Practical Guide
Rashid N. Khan

*Business Process Management is a Team Sport:
Play it to Win!*
Andrew Spanyi

*The Death of 'e' and the Birth of the
Real New Economy*
Peter Fingar and Ronald Aronica

Enterprise E-Commerce
Peter Fingar, Harsha Kumar and Tarun Sharma

MK
Meghan-Kiffer Press
Tampa, Florida, USA
www.mkpress.com
Innovation at the Intersection of Business and Technology